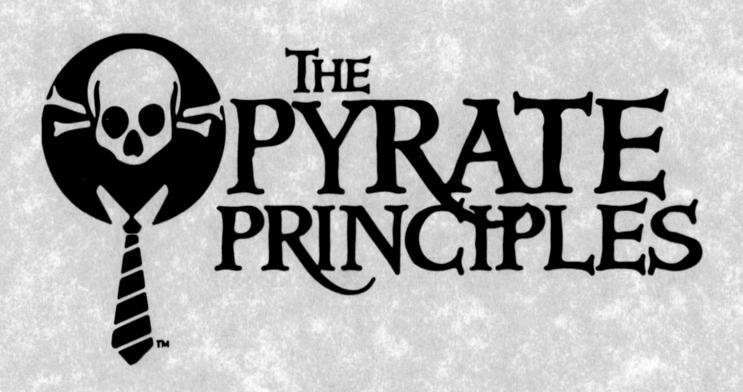

The Pyrate Principles™

Legendary Keys to Transform Your Life, Business, or Organization

Steve Monroe

Designed by Brian Wilson Sykes

Illustrations by Nicolas David Miller Sykes

Library of Congress Cataloging-in-Publication Data:
Monroe, Steve 1946—
The Pyrate Principles™ Legendary Keys to Transform Your Life, Business, or Organization/Monroe, Steve.
p. cm.
Includes bibliographic references.
1. Edward Teach, d. 1718 2. Pirates—North Carolina---Colonial America--Caribbean, 3. History—18th Century

ISBN 978-0-9791337-3-2

Printed in the United States of America on acid-free paper that meets the American National Standards Institute Z 39-48 Standard.

ABolderImage
Action Printing - Ad Press

ABolder Image / Ad Press
205 Aloe Road
Greensboro NC 27409
336.856.1300

First Edition
10 9 8 7 6 5 4 3 2 1

Acknowledgements

The author would like to thank,

Louise Monroe, who, after twenty-five years of hearing about Blackbeard, is thrilled that it is completed to her standards.

Sari Steinberg, who has caused me to go deep and keep writing, and her co-conspirator, Abigail Pickus, who asked great questions of the text and the author.

Haia R'nana Bchiri's invaluable contribution gave new meaning to the text and Principles.

Lindsey Cox, who did the initial editing until family got more important, and stayed around to clear up the final draft.

Keri Covert, a most versatile member of my crew, reading, editing, calling, organizing, co-presenting, selling, and keeping me sane.

Jessica Harman, a co-presenter and sales professional, whose compassion came through in her interviews and was a continued voice of encouragement to the author.

Andy Lindsay, proud grandfather, early listener, creator of the Pyrate Principles™ logo, and master filmmaker.

Brian Sykes, all things digital and designer of the cover, who laid out the book and whose creative light is always on.

Nicolas Sykes, for his illustrations that brought added life to The Principles.

Annisa Jean Monroe, who keeps me focused on what is really important and keeps the bills paid.

Grandsons **Heath Robert Benton Monroe** and **Bryce David Welder**, who love all things pirate and supplied some great ideas.

Cathy Chesney, who was among the first to believe and gave shape to the idea.

Julia Smith, who added dimension to the text in spectacular fashion.

Cheryl Collins, the model of Executive Officers of organizations, who is a dear friend with a great ear and a bigger heart.

Jim Venable, **Cliff Barrett**, and **Eddie Oakley**, the guys at the Jamestown Y, who have heard more about Blackbeard than they care to know.

Cody Byrd pioneer co-presenter, committed custom-home builder and home building leader, and part-time pirate.

James Dodson, husband, father, pretty good golfer, and awesome author, who is my inspiration when sitting in front of a blank screen.

Dr. Nido Qubein, who listened early and provided great advice to a novice author/speaker.

The gang at the **Greensboro Farmer's Market**, who continue to inquire and spur on my efforts, **Carman** and **Charles**, **Alicia**, **Lisa**, **Cheryl**, **Josie**, **Susanne**, and **Judy**, the persistent.

ABolder Image Printing professionals, **John**, **Ruth**, and **Chris**, **Julie**, **Jeff**, **Joe** and **Rob** for getting the book on and off the press in good time.

Mike McGervey, steady hand at the controls of Life Coaching and websites, who has seen and heard it all and only keeps the good parts.

Blythe Leonard, artist and entrepreneur, modeling creativity and caring in an emerging generation.

Sara Eller and **Guardian Building Products** for allowing the Pyrate Principles™ a national forum initially to present the Principles.

Robin Williams, who has been the consistent voice in my head and heart, keeping me on course.

Sherry Pinney-Phillips for unleashing the leadership power of the Pyrate Principles™ to organizations.

Randy Noel, Chairperson of the **National Association of Home Builders**, who lives leadership everyday and inspires an industry in changing times.

Desiree Wall who did initial company research.

Dedication

The book is dedicated to the memory and legacy of **Carl Robert Monroe**. Husband, father, grandfather, brother, uncle, friend, and golfer. He was a faithful follower and servant of Christ.

Proceeds

Proceeds from this book will go to support:

Scholarships at **Georgetown College**, Georgetown, Kentucky

Scholarships at **High Point University**, High Point, North Carolina

Leadership development at **Pi Kappa Alpha Foundation.**

Mike Rowe WORKS Foundation, educating young people in vital trades.

Market Place® with **Kai Ryssdal,** an incredible daily business news program.

Table of Contents

Pyrate Principles:

Introduction

Winds whipped the sails as the captain steered the ship starboard, framed by a clear midnight sky unpolluted by city lights. Bathed in moonlight, the crew scrambled across the deck, balancing on a bow rocked by powerful waves as the music swelled. I stood amid this picturesque scene, suddenly cast into Treasure Island, the beloved book of my childhood, or the precious original Pirates of the Caribbean movies. A rush of ocean breeze carried with it a yet-unknown clarity; the stars sparkled above as I set my course for my next adventure, accompanied by the spirits of the Brethren of the Coast, pirates who once navigated the sea beneath me and whose wisdom can serve as a compass for those of us attempting to traverse the stormy seas of the world we live in.

Upon my return to shore, I found myself walking the same streets as the notorious Captain Blackbeard. I strode through Ocracoke, the island that served as Blackbeard's haven and his final headquarters, and stumbled upon a small bookstore. There I began to arm myself with as much knowledge as I could about the bygone Golden Age of piracy and the man who stood at the helm of its flagship, his ebony beard and crisscrossed cutlasses striking fear into the hearts of anyone who dared to draw near his dear Queen Anne's Revenge. I dove deeper and deeper into the myths and truths surrounding those who once sailed under the Jolly Roger, deliberately transforming inwardly and outwardly as I immersed myself in their tales.

Drawn again and again to the shores that once served as an oasis for my dramatically-dressed muse, a gradual change emerged in me, intensifying with each visit to the island, each new fact I added to my horde, each new jewel of a book I unearthed. I sifted through slander and silliness, shedding Hollywood's glorified and demonized picture of pirates to reveal a clear, honest one, one that I had come to reflect physically (though, restraining my mirroring of my bygone brethren, perhaps not to the same extreme as my melodramatic muse). Gone was the mild-mannered, button-down business type, replaced by a long-haired seafarer with an unquenchable thirst for knowledge and a mind churning with greater intensity than an ocean in a storm.

On one of my voyages into the past, I found my treasure at last. Allowing my mind to wander, an idea took the form of a dusty, forgotten volume buried at the bottom of a box, beneath other boxes, of books on piracy. On the sparse, time-worn pages, a strong hand had once scrawled the tricks of his trade, his business. Between the fading, gilded covers lay the lasting lessons Blackbeard had learned from his mentor, Ben Hornigold, and the weathered wisdom of Blackbeard himself. Armed with these newfound "Pyrate Principles," I began to steer the insight of the infamous pirate into its contemporary applications.

And so this book was born where the past flows into the present, where the sea of the wisdom of the ages meets the pool of knowledge that I have amassed in my time at the helm.

A Brief Note on Blackbeard

One day around 1680, a baby boy came screaming into the world, perhaps gracing a Bristol home, perhaps opening his eyes for the first time in a house in Jamaica. Whatever his roots, the boy once known as Edward Teach grew strong and bold, earning his sea legs in the Royal Navy aboard a sixty-gun frigate during Queen Anne's War. Called back to the sea after his service, Teach found a mentor and captain in Ben Hornigold.

The year 1717 found Teach shedding his subservience and building a new name for himself, based on his natural gifts, the whiskers on his face, and his flair for the theatrical. The student broke away from his mentor and became captain in his own right aboard his ship, Queen Anne's Revenge. So began two years of terror, as the man henceforth known as Blackbeard quickly took command of the sea, capturing forty ships and a skiff, holding a major southern port for ransom, and laying the foundation for what he hoped would be a new pirate haven in Ocracoke. Blackbeard's reign began when, in October of 1717, he ravaged the Mid-Atlantic coast from the Capes of Delaware to New York Harbor and then down to Chesapeake as no one ever had before. Fifteen vessels fell prey to this new, mighty captain, a man who became a myth nearly overnight (1). Tall, lean, and armed to the teeth, Blackbeard made a fiery impression with his great black beard aflame in battle. He was a force to be reckoned with, yet he was not known for actual violence. The captain of the Queen Anne's Revenge was clever, strong, and fearsome, but his reign required no bloodshed until the bloody battle that raged on the day he fell. Not only that, but he was fiercely loyal to his fellow pirates, as seen when he wrought revenge on the East Coast following the death of his friend Samuel "Black Sam" Bellamy, the "Prince of Pirates."

The notion that he was so "giving" with his fellow pirates that he passed around his wife for his crew's enjoyment is nothing but pure balderdash. He was no different from other men of power in his practice of keeping his treasures close – not to mention the fact that there is no record of any of Blackbeard's wives going to sea with him and violating the seafarers' common code (famously broken by one pirate captain) forbidding women aboard, lest the ship be struck with bad luck. On shore, Blackbeard did not shy away from ladies: his attractiveness amplified by his great fame and fortune, he found favor in the eyes of several wives – for a time, at least. Blackbeard's last marriage was to the sixteen-year-old daughter of a wealthy family from Bath Towne, North Carolina. (Of course, in Blackbeard's day, his young bride's age would have stirred up no scandal and a handsome man double her age would have been considered a great catch, if her family didn't mind his pirating ways).

What family name and country of origin should have appeared on his myriad of marriage certificates remains a mystery. Some say he was Edward Thatch or Teach of Jamaica, or of Bristol (2). Others cast him as the son of an unknown wealthy aristocrat and slave owner in Spanish Town, Jamaica (3). Yet others claim the seafarer's land of origin as Bermuda (4). Some go so far as to besmirch the captain's creativity and the fame of his midnight-black facial hair by claiming that his nickname was little more than a derivation of his possible family name, Black. Kevin P. Duffus (in his The Last Days of Black Beard the Pirate) asserts that it is the other half of Blackbeard's nickname that lacks originality since he was the son of James Beard, neighbor of Charles Eden and Tobias Knight, who were destined to return to the boy's story many years later. Whatever life Blackbeard once had on land, he cast it off when he took to the seas, the truth of it perhaps lost with the diary and ship's log he was known to keep (a few pages of which were reprinted in the Boston News Letter after falling into the hands of Lt. Robert Maynard upon their author's demise. Most were said to be lost to the ages).

In control of the Queen Anne's Revenge, the Adventure, and at times even a few lesser-known vessels, Blackbeard was truly due the title of "commodore." Disregarding the proper maritime titles of their subject, imperial authorities and newspapers in his time – and later, Hollywood – have clung to their demonized "Captain Blackbeard," and so he is known. Literate, young, and clever, Blackbeard found allies in North Carolina Governor

Charles Eden and his Chief Justice, Tobias Knight. The infamous pirate captain even managed to receive the King's pardon in the form of his Act of Grace in 1718; however, even with all of these merits, Blackbeard could not escape his tragic fall.

Hounded by Lieutenant Governor Alexander Spotswood of Virginia, Blackbeard ran the Queen Anne's Revenge aground near present-day Beaufort, North Carolina, and took a crew of fifteen sailors with him aboard the smaller Adventure. Nonetheless, Spotswood would not be mollified, his ceaseless pursuit perhaps motivated by a yearning to protect colonial Virginia, perhaps by less noble reasons: might he have been jealous that his fellow governor had grown rich thanks to his alliance with Blackbeard? Blameless hero or corrupt politician, Spotswood's tireless chase climaxed in Blackbeard's final battle with the Royal Navy. Despite the warnings of Tobias Knight, whose ill-gotten booty had been discovered by Spotswood's forces in their attempt to raid the pirate's home and capture him on shore, Blackbeard found himself face to face with his dogged pursuer.

And so Blackbeard and a number of his crew went down to "meet Davy Jones" (one of many colorful pirate terms for dying), and several survived the battle only to meet their ends at the bottom of a rope. A few escaped, including one William Howard, who made Ocracoke Island his home, as the fallen captain had once wished it to be for all pirates. The once-feared, forever-remembered captain fell near his beloved Ocracoke on November 22, 1718, after a mere two years commanding the seas. In those two years, he accomplished more than many seafarers did in far longer lifetimes, passing through into immortality despite his short stay on earth.

Unpacking the Treasure Chest of Myths and Mysteries Surrounding the Brethren of the Coast

Unfurl your sails and let the winds of time sweep you back centuries, back to a time before Hollywood gave the seafarers once known as "pyrates" a devilish makeover, and new spelling standards gave them an "i." Sail back to the reign of Queen Elizabeth I, when Her Majesty herself invested her trust and her money in the pirating Sir Francis Drake as he sailed around the world to bring her kingdom great wealth (5). Back to the sixteen-hundreds, when merchants in colonial America were wont to hire pirates to take out their foreign competition. Back to the seventeenth and eighteenth centuries, when pirates were royally ordained to attack any vessel from a land not their own. Back to when pirates often found themselves known as "privateers."

The difference? In an age when war and exploration dominated the minds of monarchs and merchants, a ship and crew who cared not for restrictive laws came in handy. With war looming on the horizon, the crowned heads of Europe commissioned crews to take on specifically Spanish, French, or Dutch ships, sharing the profits of their adventures with their royal employers and occasionally doing away with a member of the former's navy. The privateers made a monetary profit and were left to plunder unprosecuted while the kings and queens added to the royal coffers and had their dirty work done without risk of a single scratch to the ships of their royal navies. While privateers were not guaranteed to avoid the ships of their land of employ, they were known to deliberately target their country's enemies. Racing for control of the New World and thus weighed down with gold, silver, and ancient artwork, the Spanish found themselves at the mercy of English privateers so often that on a number of occasions Spain sent ambassadors to approach the Crown in protest. They were ignored in the most polite English fashion.

Privateers could emerge even without a royal edict: typically law-abiding merchants in the Thirteen Colonies were apt to sponsor ships of privateers, going so far at times as to build a ship, hire a captain, and entrust that captain with the task of assembling a crew. These ships would take to the seas and seek out merchantmen of different nationalities, board their rigs, and rob them of their cargo. Upon their return to shore, the privateers would turn over eighty percent of their profits to their sponsors, thus serving the merchants a dual purpose: eliminating competition and being a source of income in their own right. Not only that, but the sponsoring merchants would then turn around a sell the privateers – at full retail! – the supplies they needed for their next voyage, generating even more profit in the process. And while the privateers may not have been the richest of men, they were free to sail the open seas and ply their trade without fear of the hempen halter (pirate-speak for the hangman's noose).

It was not long, however, before the tides changed and colonial ministers began to press their congregations to put a stop to the evil practices of the privateers (never, of course, mentioning the involvement of the merchants who were no doubt generous supporters of the church). Legitimate sea captains, enraged at the loss of their ships and prone to exaggerate the wickedness of their pirate attackers in order to boost their own reputations, aided in sparking the privateer witch hunt (6).

All this animosity toward privateers crashed up against the wave of seamen seeking jobs after the War of Spanish Succession ended in 1714 and the Royal Navy no longer had a need for them. Within two years, the navy reduced its ranks from 49,860 men to a mere 13,475 (7). What is a man who knows of nothing but the sea and combat to do? The law of supply and demand was certainly not working in their favor: with the surplus of available help, legitimate employers hired only the most experienced of sailors, which often meant hiring the older, stricter seamen, leading to a sharp increase in discipline at sea (8). Thus adventure-seeking seafarers were further discouraged from finding employment on the now far less free vessels of their day. To add insult to injury, experienced and inexperienced sailors alike saw their wages drop fifty percent between 1707 and 1714.

1713 to 1715 became a brief eye in the storm of

unemployment as merchants required a large number of seamen to transport goods to extended trade routes, but this only led to a worsened employment slump that continued until the 1730s. So where did that leave countless able-bodied, often younger sailors with no chance – or perhaps even desire – to work aboard legitimate vessels with harsh discipline and low wages? Keeping a weather eye on the horizon for the best opportunity they could find, the fogs of frustration and failure to find employment lifted, and their opportunity took on a clear, corporeal form. Piracy. Relieved of any contract but the pirate codes they themselves wrote and signed freely, seamen set sail for their own gain, chasing the horizon of their newfound opportunities.

And so the Brethren of the Coast was born.

No longer bound to take what the merchants wanted and give most of it back to their employers, these pirates shifted their focus to a different sort of booty. Unwelcome at most ports, pirates had no choice but to sustain themselves through theft. They developed a penchant for stealing supplies from captured ships. For instance, in 1717 the merchant ship Restoration found itself under attack by pirates and robbed of gear such as needles, long-lines, pumps, sails, twine, a kettle, and a frying pan (9). Similarly, in 1723 the sloop Content met with a similar fate, their pirate attackers confiscating an ill-begotten haul including boxes of soap and candles in addition to a flying-jib, a flying-jib boom, and flying-jib-halliards (a rope used to raise or lower sails and flags), an anchor, tools for carpentry, cable, and main halliards (10).

Contrary to the image of bloodthirsty scallywags portrayed in motion pictures, pirates were not known for engaging in much more violence than raising a red or black flag and giving their target a shot across the bow (11). The very infamy of pirates in itself was enough to strike fear into the heart of any savvy captain, who would promptly surrender without necessitating any bloodshed. Easily boarding the ships of cowed captains, pirates could take what they wanted, give nothing back, and never dirty their hands with blood. Such was the power of pirates during their Golden Age.

So great was their influence that some theorize that pirates may have had a hand in geopolitical drama between imperialist forces battling it out in the Caribbean, along the Spanish Main, and as far as the Pacific coast of the still-colonial Americas (12). Most pirates kept primarily to the Caribbean, making names for themselves off the coasts of Barbados, Jamaica, and other islands while often returning to the pirate haven of New Providence, Bermuda.

The Republic of Pirates, as it was known, may not have been granted the same magical myth that writers of later centuries bestowed upon the former pirate haven Tortuga, nor does it bear the same fame as its mysterious neighbor, the Bermuda Triangle. But to pirates, it was an oasis in the stormy waters of persecution. It was said that when "a pirate slept, he didn't dream he'd died and gone to heaven, he dream[t] that he once again returned to New Providence" (13). Then the capital of the British Bahamas, New Providence was not free of royal rule, but governors were easily bribed to ignore the illegal activity happening right beneath their proper noses.

A port to call home was necessary, especially as Woodes Rogers arrived on the shores of once-heavenly New Providence and began to administer the King's Act of Grace in 1717. Those who took advantage of the Act of Grace were pardoned for past offenses. Those who did not surrender the lifestyle of and their loyalty to the Brethren of the Coast were tracked down, captured, and sent en masse to dance the hempen jig.

The British government had officially decided that it was time to rob the Golden Age of its glimmer. British authorities in the islands and the colonies cracked down on piracy. Ben Hornigold, the legendary former captain and mentor of Blackbeard, led the charge that was steadily hunting down and hanging crew after crew of pirates. The number of pirates sailing free dwindled as the crew of Davy Jones's Flying Dutchman grew, and before long the Golden Age of piracy itself was sent to the Locker.

Format of the Book

The book is laid out in chapters according to the seventeen Pyrate Principles contained therein. The language of Blackbeard's day is preserved in the notes for the initial section of each chapter. The second part, called "Bonus Brethren Information," is comprised of examples and explanations expounding on the use (or damaging disuse) of the principle by other Golden Age pirates. The third section, "Application," is an example of individuals and companies I have come across, captains of industry, who stand as models of these positive principles and carry them out during our time (with an emphasis on products and services that are made or offered in the United States). A fourth part of each chapter is a short offering of thought questions to help readers better focus on or deal with what they have just read and utilize it most wisely as a navigational tool for their lives, businesses, or organizations.

While none of the companies or individuals in these chapters may aspire to be pirates in the usual use of the term, they, like the enterprising seafarers of old, are inspirational and are transforming their worlds. They are creating jobs and building organizations that reshape their communities. It has been my privilege to interview and interact with many of these captains during the research stage of compiling this book. Like the sun bursting through the clouds and mists over a stormy sea, they have brightened many a day for me as I gathered up the treasures of their stories. In reading this book, you will discover men and women of vision, purpose, passion, and clarity of mission. Be prepared to be inspired, and perhaps engage your own inner-pirate, to have a positive impact on your world.

Aye, welcome aboard and good sailing.

Know Yer Home Waters and Use That Knowledge to Yer Advantage

I

Only the most experienced and daring sailors want to go on account as a part of me crew. They know the waters around the principal islands of the Caribbean and Pamlico Sound better than Poseidon himself. We thus can be navigating at night or in a storm, much to the surprise of some fat merchant vessels that are thus pushed into the Sound by Ignorance, Greed, or the unpredictable winds.

When those swinish fribbles' lookouts see that it is the Queen Anne's Revenge that pursues 'em, they try and scurry for the protection of the center of the Sound. As they head for the Sound, they will soon find that the twenty-five (mile) width is often five fathoms deep or less. We wait and enjoy the drama as they run themselves aground, surrounded by hundreds of square miles of open water, often without wasting a single shot. Some of the more enterprising members of me crew wager on where and when the merchant will ground.

Bonus Brethren Information

While Blackbeard was writing about the area around Ocracoke and what he may have seen as the future of pirates and others in that territory, he and his crew plied the waters considerably south. Areas such as the Straits of Florida and the Windward Passage carried ships laden with goods from Europe or captive, slaves from Africa. Pirates knew these waters well. Much to the delight and profit of pirates, Spanish sea captains did not do well off the Florida coast in a hurricane July 30-31, 1715. Eleven ships, part of Spain's Tierra Firme fleet, with tons of gold, were lost to the surf and coast line. Pirates followed the disaster by standing off shore and diving for the gold.

::: APPLICATION :::

Munroe Dairy

A little ways off from the banks of the Seekonk River lies the small town of Rumford, Rhode Island, home of a mere 8,176 souls, including relatives of mine. On one of my journeys to visit my family, while strolling along a golf course with my wife, we came upon a large truck with the distinctive markings of a Holstein cow. Had Ben and Jerry's begun making home deliveries?

The puzzle remained unsolved for a number of days, until at last we were able to approach the mysterious vessel and read the name "Munroe Dairy" printed along its side. Further inquiries with our kin revealed that Munroe Dairy, unencumbered by twenty-first-century norms, delivers fresh milk and related products directly to the doors of local homes. Such practices harkened back to my childhood in central Kentucky, where I recall a milkman delivering to our back door – but that was "a few" years back. To add to the peculiarity, the business that already should have been shark bait last millenium had been named Business of the Year by the East Providence Chamber of

Commerce as recently as 2015.

The mists of mystery seemed to grow thicker the more I learned, and so I sought to part them by setting out to meet Lindsey Armstrong Mitchell, Munroe Dairy's director of marketing and public relations. Acting that day as my personal guide, Lindsey revealed that she is the daughter of the current owner, Rob Armstrong, who took over the business from his father in 1988. Though no longer the property of the same dynasty that founded it in 1881 (having passed from the Munroes to the Armstrongs in 1936), Munroe Dairy remains a family business, the helm of which is handed over from generation to generation along with the secrets to its success. To Lindsey's way of thinking, the keys to the treasure that is Munroe Dairy are its outstanding employees and its equally remarkable customers.

Munroe Dairy has 12,000 loyal customers scattered across three states (and they are about to raise that number as they edge into Boston). Every day, Munroe workers gather milk from nearby dairies, pasteurize it, and deliver it to homes – all within forty-eight hours or fewer and all with phenomenal customer service. By contrast, dairies that serve chain food stores may take several days to receive, process, and deliver their product to the stores, where it then sits on a refrigerated shelf waiting for the customer to come and get it. For Munroe Dairy, the process is personal, and as a result they have a unique understanding of their consumers. They have charted their territory and learned it better than their competitors, giving them Blackbeard's advantage. Additionally, they know the lay of the land where their trucks "make port," and have thus expanded their business to offer over two hundred items, many of which they pick up from local producers and deliver to the doors of their treasured customers.

Ever on top of the changing tides of trends, Munroe Dairy sends out monthly flyers that promote its expanded product line and feature a nonprofit organization or cause to which they donate a portion of profits from a certain product. The Munroe crew also is learning to navigate social media and establishing a stronger and stronger presence there. Customers receive weekly email reminders, birthday messages, and electronic notices about new product offerings. There are daily posts on the company's Facebook page, and an active presence on Twitter and Pinterest. The Munroe hands keep their website updated and overflowing with information on the company, its history, and well-made videos from area dairy farmers with whom they hold long-term relationships.

Munroe Dairy has made an Ocracoke out of its business, creating a home base in its plant that has operated in the same place for the past one hundred thirty-five years and providing loyal support not only internally, but also for other brethren – local food suppliers and local family-owned farms. None of Munroe Dairy's milk comes from huge factory farms, nor is it adulterated with additives, stabilizers, or synthetics, nor is it even ultra-pasteurized; the company's philosophy is that the less handled and processed milk is, the better its taste and the more nutritious it is for consumers.

Munroe Dairy's devoted crew members also have committed themselves to maintaining their unique perspective and hold on their territory. When Rob Armstrong's father retired, Rob seriously considered weighing anchor and closing the company for good. But the crew stood steadfast, beginning their days at two in the morning and doubling their delivery routes in order to expand their turf without losing ground that they already held. The sacrifices of the crew did not go unnoticed, and their captain, Rob, credits them with the continued success of the company. The tireless efforts and friendly manner of the crew allow customers to put great trust in Munroe Dairy, staying true to the business and keeping it afloat. Customers even go so far as to leave their doors open so that delivery drivers may enter, drop off their product, and check to see if the home is missing anything else from the broad array of products they provide.

For a hundred thirty-five years, the leadership and employees of Munroe Dairy have maintained a keen understanding of their territory and used it to their advantage. Blackbeard would have been proud to have their products delivered to his port.

Unleashing the Inner Pyrate in Your World:

What lessons could you learn from this regional captain of industry that has set itself apart from its larger competitors?

1.

2.

What do you need to make it happen in your world?

When will you do it?

Don't Keep All That Ye Capture—Let them Go Who Would Enhance Yer Image

II

There be several myths at sea about me, Blackbeard. One is that no one ever escapes me grasp. 'Tis not true.

I only take booty that I can barter, sell, or use for provisions and weapons or to reward me loyal crew fer their labour. Hostages be rare, and vessels, with the exception of the Queen Anne's Revenge and the sturdy sloop Adventure, be not worth keeping. Why drag behind yer vessel anything that would slow ye down or keep ye from responding to danger or another opportunity?

We do from time to time capture a vessel that has aboard a comely lass or a blustering gentleman and make examples of them, as I did in Charles Towne. I bottled up the harbour and kept a counselman aboard until the lily-livered leaders of the city complied with me wishes.

What I did in Charles Towne harbor makes the point. I stopped and plundered merchantmen (9). Kept a most prominent member of the towne aboard as I sent two crew members ashore with me demands and instructions regarding what I wanted in return. All prisoners were threatened and I was angered more than once by the sluggishness of the towne to respond. No one was brought to harm, but they took with 'em harrowing stories in their imaginations to enthrall and entertain family and friends for generations.

Charm fer the ladies and, a'course, humiliation and intimidation fer the men work well. When the captured be set free, they shall talk. A live witness is better than ten keeping company with Davy Jones.

Bonus Brethren Information

Captain Thomas White, an educated sailor-turned-pirate from Plymouth, embodied this principle before Blackbeard even began his reign of the seas. White was smart and savvy, having escaped slavery and even death (including a plot on his life) on more than one occasion.

On one of his voyages, White and his men seized an entire ship, including the crew, as pirates were wont to do. The captured men who refused to join White's pirate crew were not harmed, but rather set free on shore and even allowed to take with them any books, papers, and personal effects that belonged to them (1). Unbelievably, White and his men even left their freed prisoners with several casks of liquor and weapons (including powder) so that they would be able to survive and purchase provisions on the foreign shore whereupon they had been set down.

On another of his adventures, White discovered that one of his men had taken some spoons (likely silver) belonging to children aboard the ship they had just plundered. He swiftly lectured his men and demanded that the children's possessions be returned promptly. The crew obeyed and, moreover, gave the children around one hundred and twenty dollars to boot (2)! And so the pirate White had less blood and silver on his ledger, but was far richer in fame.

::: APPLICATION :::

National Speakers' Association and Off-Campus Writers' Workshop

Like the savvy pirates of the past, there are those in this millennium with great gifts who choose not to keep all that they capture. Two organizations come to mind.

The National Speakers' Association (NSA) was founded in 1973 by Cavett Robert of Mississippi. He soon amassed a crew of women and men who wanted, as he did, to set a higher standard for speakers and presenters across the country. They seem to be succeeding in their endeavor with over thirty-five hundred members and thirty-five state and regional chapters.

One of the tenets of their code is to encourage others who may want to become professional speakers to hone their craft, spurred on by those already sailing the steadier waters of success. They engender an openness to receive even the most inexperienced speakers and take them aboard in order to "build a bigger pie" and expand the horizons of the field. They do not hoard their knowledge and lock it away in treasure chests to be buried and lost with them, but rather they, like Blackbeard, give others a chance to tell their tales.

Often held monthly, local chapter meetings exemplify this spirit of sharing. At a typical meeting, successful speakers or presenters are brought in to demonstrate their craft with a typical talk. This may take the form of a presentation; a keynote; keys to being an effective consultant, humorist, motivator, or author; or the leading of a workshop. After the talk draws to a close, the general audience can invoke its own form of parlay and ask questions of this captain of the field. Other specific NSA members offer suggestions to the one presenting.

The next section of the meeting takes on teaching to the task. During the subsequent lunch break, participants can network and form fleets of important connections, all the while sharing insights and ideas like a cask of rum. Following lunch, the same or another professional speaker may take the helm. Great content is shared either way. Like their pirate predecessors, the members of the NSA know the power of speech and its capacity to spread and cause change. They understand that giving people the tools and freedom to speak is truly to their benefit, even if giving away the treasures of their trade does not seem immediately profitable.

Another group that grants voices to those it encounters is the Off-Campus Writers' Workshop (OCWW). Founded in 1946, it is said to be the oldest such organization in the United States, a New Providence for Chicago-area writers seeking a haven where their voices can flourish. The first mate and quartermaster of this book – two of its editors – have been participants in the group for over a decade, one of them even serving on its board for a time.

OCWW meetings are held weekly from September through May, from 9:30 to 12:00 on Thursday mornings at the Winnetka Community House in a northern suburb of Chicago. At each meeting, a different speaker takes command: successful writers, editors, and publishers unpack before the participants their treasure troves of insights, prompts, and writing-process techniques. Their wisdom speaks to writers across genres, from mystery to romance to script-writing to travel columns and beyond, and across levels of experience. In fact, participants span everyone from newbies just gaining their sea legs and hoping to fulfill lifelong ambitions of writing to best-selling authors coming back into port to add more skills to their professional cache before testing the waters anew. Topics range from interview skills to writing dialogue to honing an "elevator pitch" to creating dynamic characters. Every spring, OCWW's Editors' Day draws crowds who wish to hear what traditional publishers want to see in a submission or what the pros and cons are of sponsoring their own ships by self-publishing.

During a regular session, the first half is typically devoted to a presentation and the second half to speaker-led manuscript critiques in which a previously submitted piece is read anonymously and all those present can offer praise and suggestions for improvement. In the end, the writer of the piece may step forward and reveal his or her identity or remain in the shadows and sail on anonymously with new critiques in hand. Between segments of each session, participants sheathe their pens, share their new publishing accomplishments, and congratulate each other on their successes. Members also have a chance to fly their flags and network by means of a directory and list serve.

Despite the dangers of sharing one's priceless wisdom and unpublished work, the participants and presenters of OCWW trust that the others present won't scuttle their ships and steal their secrets for themselves. It is this spirit of camaraderie that allows all who attend to share their hard-won spoils without risk of being marooned without their scribe's supplies, their stories safe from greedy hands. They need not fear competition or plagiarism: all participants and presenters obey an unspoken code of conduct and take only what they need in the form of lessons, critiques, and insights, leaving all to sail on – unharmed – with more stories to tell.

Unleashing the Inner Pyrate in Your World:

This principle has two excellent examples of organizations that take, give, and share justly in a variety of ways.

When you look at your business or organization, what ideas come through that will enhance your name among those you serve?

1.

2.

What do you need to make it happen in your world?

When will you do it?

Be Distinctive In Yer Personal Style and Presentation

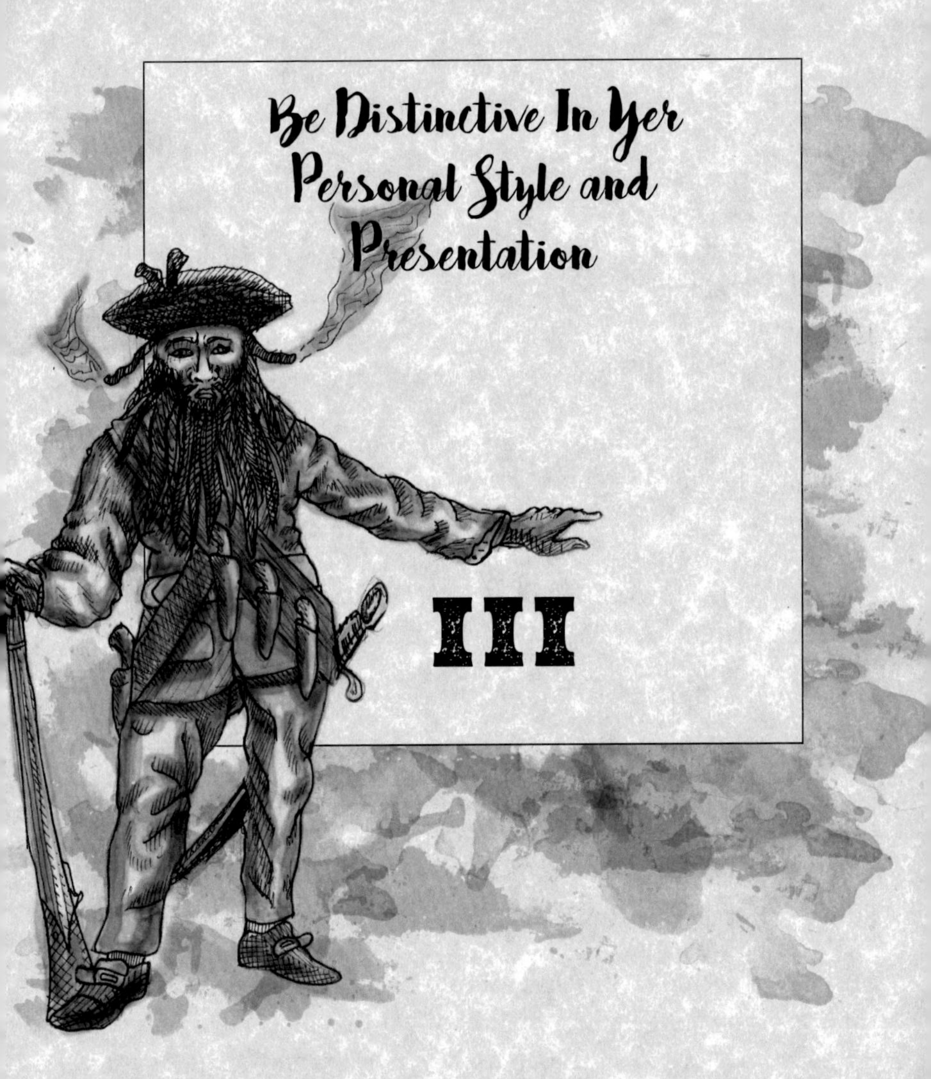

III

Ye have no doubt seen the woodcuts of me that have been run in newsbooks. Why d'ye think I wear me hair the way I do, with the cluster of smoke that flows from me beard, or the six pistols crisscrossed? Fer me health? I must wash following every raid, jist to get the stench of gunpowder out.

But whatever ships run afoul of me, they know they have been sacked and captured by Blackbeard. Not sure who gave me that name, but one day I ought to track down his miserable carcass and thank him. Those mangy curs on shore will print most anything to sell newsbooks. The be soe starved fer a story that they believe whate'er they hear and exaggerate the rest about much of what me and me crew do. All the better: those foolish landlubbers jist aid in me efforts to plant fear in the hearts of men.

Bonus Brethren Information

Pirate Captain Bartholomew "Black Bart" Roberts was a grand example of a man who knew the value of style. He has been reported to dress most flamboyantly, clad head to toe in the color of blood, with a crimson waistcoat and matching breeches. He adorned his hat grandly with a feather, in the aristocratic fashion of the day. Around his neck hung a great golden chain weighed down by a cross of glittering diamonds. He armed himself with a magnificent sword as well as two pairs of pistols, which hung from silk slings that were flung over his well-dressed shoulders. Black Bart boldly dressed to impress, and his efforts paid off richly: in his days at the helm, Black Bart's Royal Fortune captured and plundered some four hundred ships (1).

::: APPLICATION :::

American-Produced Clothing and Accessories

Carried to us steadily on the winds of time, the old adage "dress to impress" still rings truer than a well-aimed cannon shot. The definition of the saying, however, has changed with the tides. While some captains of industry and their crews, and the occasional civilian setting out to woo a mate, still don formal or business-formal clothes, the norm in the twenty-first-century has shifted to business casual. Chic dresses or eye-catching shirts with wrinkle-resistant trousers are the new crimson waistcoats. Gold chains and diamond crosses have been replaced by leather belts, stylish handbags, and the occasional matching sport coat. While styles vary from workplace to workplace and person to person, one element unites all of their clothes: they sport labels.

All clothing has history. Perhaps the history of a pair of pants is less enthralling than that of a pair of pistols, but it holds a great power. Textile companies affix labels to their products in their own understated but clear way of dressing not only their customers, but their clothes themselves, to impress.

In the Piedmont area of North Carolina where I have weighed anchor and docked, three industries once dominated like the Queen Anne in the Caribbean. The third such industry is textiles manufacturing. The Piedmont once boasted textiles of every conceivable shape, texture, and color, from bloody crimson to royal violet. The flagship of that industry was denim. Although conceived and birthed in America, much denim manufacturing has since been moved offshore. Still, those with plenty of pieces of eight (money by any other name will smell as sweet) can still purchase a pair of custom jeans woven on the ancient looms at Cone Mills in Greensboro, North Carolina. Unlike mass-produced jeans, this pricey pair will last a lifetime due to improved manufacturing processes and thicker fabric.

And what should a present-day pirate sport with a label boasting the worth of a three hundred seventy-five dollar pair of jeans? What else but a tasteful golf shirt.

The tide is rising steadily for the ubiquitous golf shirt, the new unofficial uniform of more progressive offices and the world of IT. Admittedly, I myself have been caught up in this tide; I have a closet chock full of golf shirts. As a captain of marketing, over the years I found myself solicited by a fleet of suppliers who plied me with golf shirts branded, like a captured pirate, with a variety of logos. The branding that mattered most to me, though, was that which lay beneath the surface of the outer layer. Peeking at the labels, I made a curious discovery. If one were to lay out a map and place a pin in every country that manufactures these shirts, one would find that one country remained unpinned. My home port lay bare on a map with pins spreading to the four corners of the earth.

Then, on a recent brief voyage to merchants near my house, I discovered my elusive treasure: a golf shirt made in the U.S.A! Not only that, but this rare shirt had been manufactured in the state Blackbeard and I both called home. Impressed by the "Made in America" label in which the shirt was dressed, I set off to trace its origins.

The journey from raw materials to shirt on a store shelf begins with cotton. In this case, the cotton is not shipped across the ocean from Southeast Asia but grown in nearby Williamsburg County, South Carolina. The soil from which the cotton springs lies on the land of At McIntosh, an eighth-generation cotton farmer. The crop is harvested from October through Thanksgiving. The cotton is then picked and ginned – thanks to Eli Whitney's helpful contraption, an invention just missed by the Golden Age pirates – by Tri-County Gin in neighboring Salters, South Carolina. Free of seeds and hulls, the cotton continues its voyage, stopping next in the Piedmont and falling into the hands of the crew of Hill Spinning in Thomasville. Led by third-generation captain Mark Leonard, the mill harmoniously integrates state-of-the-art equipment with legacy equipment and thus spins the clean cotton into soft yarn.

Setting off again, the cotton makes port at the South Carolina home of White Plains Knit Fabrics in Jefferson. That company's captain, Jim Kirkley, a veteran of cotton and fabrics, keeps a portion of the material from Hill Mill to weave collars and cuffs while sending the balance to Clover Knits in Clover. There the body of the shirt is knitted and voyages back to North Carolina to be dyed. At South Fork Industries in Lincolnton, North Carolina, the material is dipped in dyes from every color of the rainbow before it is sent once again to South Carolina. Captained by Larry Crolley, Lamar-based Craig Industries is responsible for cutting, sewing, and embroidering the pieces. The finished products at last complete their journey on the shelves of various outlets, including the shop at Homegrown Cotton, under Captain At McIntosh whose polo shirts are produced locally with only natural, environmentally friendly dyes, a standard that displays a keen understanding of the value of impressing with dressing.

In an age when everything from electronics to textiles is produced offshore, a new generation has risen over the horizon and set a new course for fashion. Millennials see the worth of the impressive "Made in America" label.

San Francisco-based entrepreneur and CEO Bayard Winthrop, savvy captain of a clothing company, has observed just that and heeded it, along with Blackbeard's advice to never underestimate the value of dress (2). Winthrop's five-year-old apparel startup, American Giant, recently sailed its way into place as the darling of Slate Magazine, CNBC, and NPR's 1A for making high-quality clothing in America while keeping prices down. American Giant's twofold secret to success is far from buried; Winthrop is open about the tricks of his trade and proud to share them with the world.

Firstly, American Giant keeps all work on its own decks, cutting out the middlemen. Second, they replace the old-fashioned assembly line with a "team sew," a model that allows each member of Winthrop's crew to take responsibility for more of the product and, as a result, have a greater sense of ownership over product quality as a whole. Winthrop proclaims with pride that his factory in Middlesex, North Carolina, is crewed by happy, experienced, and thus knowledgeable men and women whom he is pleased to provide with jobs and whom he trusts to improve the product for which they make (3). Thus a label bearing "American Giant, Made in America" is one that bears with it credentials that can be quick to impress.

Blythe Leonard, a North Carolina-based leather designer, has also seen the wisdom in applying Blackbeard's principle to the Made-in-America movement. Captain of her company, Blythe Leonard LLC, which is housed in the building wherein her great-grandfather's textile dye business once made permanent port, Leonard knows the importance of buying local and supporting the economy in the land on which your company is built rather that one across the seas. She sees the direct profit of such practices for her company as well, tapping into a growing demand in America for more "transparent manufacturing," a wise business move supported by the assertions of Rajeev Batra, PhD.

A professor at the University of Michigan's Ross School of Business, Batra sees the rising tide of demand for a feeling of authenticity in their clothes, one that springs from a label bearing the ever-impressive "Made in America." Clothing companies that wish to rise to the forefront of their industry and follow Blackbeard's boat wave by impressing with dress must learn to navigate the new trend, to adapt to changing styles. The style now, it seems, is patriotic flair.

American Apparel has joined the growing fleet of companies who have begun to see the value of impressing with their dressing, their product. Working under the flag of their motto, "Ethically Made – Sweatshop Free," American Apparel has been putting American consumers to the test. They place before said customers the choice between nearly identical hoodies and t-shirts that are made either in America or across the seas. The catch is that the products made in America cost anywhere from seventeen to twenty-six percent more. The customers are ensnared like a captured ship by the ethical dilemma facing a myriad of Americans who overwhelmingly wish to support American-made products but don't want to empty their hulls by paying extra to keep the product local. Thus American consumers must decide on the relative magnitude of the value of dressing to impress and accessorizing with patriotic flair.

Unleashing the Inner Pyrate in Your World:

How can you impress potential consumers, employers, and sister businesses in the way you dress and present yourself and your business or organization?

1.

2.

What do you need to make it happen in your world?

When will you do it?

On The Decks Of Me Fleet, All Men Be Equal

IV

Whether ye be a grizzled veteran from a merchant ship, a recent escapee from one of His Majesty's men-o'-war, a captured slave seized as we boarded yer ship who's chosen to join us, or jist young and stupid with a longing for adventure and a desire to be tested, welcome aboard. How ye got here matters not.

If ye be willing to fight beside me, then ye receive an equal share of the prize when we seize her. I care not fer where ye came from, how old ye be, or the colour of yer skin. If ye be willing to work hard and risk yer life at my side in a fight, what more could I ask?

Bonus Brethren Information

There are frequent references to black pirates and their role as crew during the Golden Age. Blackbeard himself took on a multiracial crew, sixty percent of which was black, many of whom were likely British colony-born freemen (1) (2). Neither race nor nationality is mentioned in the articles or codes of any crew. Black crew members received an equal share of booty and enjoyed other benefits of crew membership, including the right to vote on board (3). Rewards and incentives appear to have been based solely on merit, untainted by racism or bigotry of any sort (4).

No pirate code or set of articles forbade black crew members from arming themselves, either, and black pirate crew members were often recorded as active combatants when they did battle alongside their shipmates (5). Black crew members even once mutinied against a tyrannical captain and his unscrupulous lackies (6). It would seem that the deck of a pirate ship was the most empowering place for a black man in the eighteenth-century white man's world (7) (8).

So colorblind were the pirate captains that Blackbeard entrusted Caesar, a former slave who was then serving aboard the Adventure, with the trying task of blowing up the captain's beloved remaining ship should the tides of his final battle turn and the vessel begin to fall into the hands of his enemies. When Blackbeard's fears of failure in the final fight were realized, English sailors scrambled below deck to find Caeser, match in hand, ready to follow his captain's last, most crucial order. Following his restraint and capture, Caeser is reputed by some to have escaped custody and lived out the rest of his life in Bath Town. Other sources have him at the end of a hempen halter with his shipmates. Either way, after his initial escape from slave owner Samuel Odell, Caeser clearly was a full-fledged, highly-trusted, equal member of Blackbeard's ill-fated crew.

Back on shore, though, the equality of a pirate vessel gave way to the racism that dominated the era. Though black and white pirates alike could meet their death at the end of a rope, captured black pirates could also be sold back into slavery. On rare occasions, a captured black pirate who could produce a "certificate of manumission" would escape slavery by qualifying for a prisoner exchange instead (9) (10). This escape option did not present itself for Blackbeard's black crew members.

When five black members of Blackbeard's crew faced the ruling council to be tried for their crimes, the question was raised whether their race lowered their status to the point where they need not be tried the same way their white shipmates were. Ultimately, though, the suggestion was cast aside and the five felt the scaffold give way beneath them, same as their white brethren. Before dancing the hempen jig, however, the captured pirates gave testimony against Tobias Knight, whose rebuttal relied on the color of the men's skin dictating the illegitimacy of their testimony. On shore, blacks were regarded as little more than chattel. Aboard a pirate ship, they were men.

::: APPLICATION :::

Rco²

One fateful day, while listening to American Public Media's "Marketplace," I discovered the company that took the pirates' once-groundbreaking idea of equality and brought it fathoms farther than anyone else in their time. Like a siren's voice rippling across the sea, Niki Okuk's interview sang through my radio and brought with it enriching enlightenment (16).

In 2012, she and her partner, Richard Carter, founded Rco² Tires in Compton, California. Armed with a noble mission, the two set out to "[save] the world twenty-two gallons at a time." To achieve this end, the company visits small- to medium-sized tire dealers and takes their trade-ins to recycle them. Each truck tire contains a buried treasure in the form of twenty-two gallons of oil, and Rco² has estimated that it has saved local landfills the equivalent of two hundred thousand gallons of oil per month. At this point, through their recycling of one million, two hundred thousand tires, the company has cleaned up a volume of oil greater than the Exxon-Valdez infamously spilled into the beautiful waters of the Prince William Sound.

Founded with the credit cards of its captains, Okuk and Carter, and a loan from the Los Angeles Jewish Free Loan Association (despite the fact that neither the company nor either of its founders has any connection to Judaism per se), Rco^2 is sailing steadily toward expanding its horizons to more rubber products or plastics or remediation. The partners' greatest triumph, the element of their company that allows them to transcend into greatness and carry the flag for Blackbeard's principle of equality, is their approach to amassing a crew. Rco^2 has thirteen employees and no background checks. And because of Okuk's progressive hiring and management practices, it provides stable jobs for local black and Latino residents who have struggled to find employment because of past criminal convictions or legal status. Aboard Okuk's ship, one's past and one's race do not matter. Everyone is human and deserves the dignity of a humane life.

Okuk, like Blackbeard, trusts her crew fully without prejudice. She believes that their work keeps the company afloat and sets their course for their next goal. On the warehouse floor, each worker has a specialized role, but everyone is also taught how to operate and fix other parts of the machinery so that work is always smooth sailing, whatever is needed. Even the foreman has first mates, a few members of the crew with a number of years of experience and training who are ready and able to step up and steer the flow of the yard should they be called upon. While Okuk is currently alone in the captain's cabin, managing all administrative elements herself, she aims to one day begin training the crew to take on her role as well. At Rco^2 neither race nor history dictates the status of a crew member. All those who serve under its flag are equal.

Unleashing the Inner Pyrate in Your World:

How have you been inspired by Rco^2 to find those who have incredible potential in your neighborhood, those who need only an opportunity to prove that they can contribute to the community?

1.

2.

What do you need to make it happen in your world?

When will you do it?

Apprenticing for the Next Cruize

V

Pyrating is great fun. Ye get to ravage, rip, and shoot people, burn and blow up for a profit. 'Tis a thrilling but dangerous life. I be always in the need of new crew to replace those who be forgetting to fight smartly.

Ye be only as good as yer poorest shot with a musket or cannon bearer when up close. Train those who be deficient in fighting skills and encourage those who lag behind. It shall save ye gathering up their bloody bodies and feeding the fish after a good fight. They need to know tryalls and how to deal with them.

By starting 'em young, ye can shape the lads into dependable crewmen and perhaps e'en a captain someday. I hear tale that Steward and Layton began in this humble manner. Look fer the keen of eye and strong of spirit. Once they have learnt the ship, a good place to start in a fight is powder monkey.

Ye may not always be met with success. I have not been, as I was not when it came to Major Stede Bonnet. Ye can only work with what they bring aboard.

Bonus Brethren Information

There was always a need for more crewmen aboard a pirate vessel. Escaped prisoners, AWOL sailors from a naval vessel looking for more money, or youngsters looking for a meal and some adventure after leaving home were all prospects for mentoring. Add to the list lads who were kidnapped by a captain or crew member and you have all the possible subjects.

For youngsters there were two primary roles wherein they could begin their lessons in piracy, neither of which was terribly promising. For one, a young pirate lad could get his start as cabin boy. Typically about fourteen to sixteen years old, the cabin boy was basically a servant of the captain and crew. He was tasked with running errands, bringing food and drink to the captain, keeping the captain's cabin tidy, doing laundry, carrying messages to crew and officers, and about a hundred other thankless tasks. Cabin boys could also become familiar with the sails, lines, and ropes and the use of each in every type of weather. They would then be sent scrambling up the rigging into the yards whenever the sails had to be trimmed. If they matured in their role and trust was established, cabin boys could go so far as to stand watches like other crewmen or act as helmsmen in good weather, even holding the wheel to keep the ship on course.

The other job available to young pirates was the powder monkey. Originally a British Naval term, this youngster, favored for his slightness of height, was pushed into service during combat, dragging bags of powder just below the gunnel to gun crews, his short stature helping him escape long gun fire from opposing vessels. Holding the most dangerous job on board, powder monkeys – if they lived – could learn the elements of being a crew member aboard the vessel. Until and unless that time came, they were universally ill-treated by other members of the crew. If his attitude was right and he was tough minded, a powder monkey could be taken under the wing of a savvy captain who would aid him in becoming a valued member of the crew.

Skilled positions such as the carpenter well may have brought and kept an apprentice aboard. The maintaining of barrels was key in keeping powder and food safe and available even in inclement climate conditions. These invaluable skills could not be properly taught ashore. The carpenter's skill with a saw was sometimes required for another, more ghastly purpose: dealing with serious wounds that could not be properly addressed by the surgeon, if the crew was even lucky enough to have one aboard.

::: APPLICATION :::

Dr. Nido Qubein, High Point University

When I weighed anchor in North Carolina twenty-four years ago to join the crew of a building-supply company as an outside sales representative, I also brought ashore a yearning to build a side career as an author and public speaker. When I shared my dream with others, I was told I would find a guide better than the North Star in Nido Qubein.

Being the shy, retiring type that I am, it took a few months for me to gather my courage and set my course for meeting Qubein, then the number-two motivational speaker in all of the United States. After several failed ventures, at last Qubein agreed to a fifteen-minute meeting that would ultimately flow into an hour-long conversation in which he charted a new course for my life. He taught me that one must use what one has written or presented in more than one medium or venue and be persistent with one's message. Someone among the ranks needs what you bring aboard.

My "Ben Hornigold" (though in my case, my mentor never turned traitor) had landed on the shores of the United States from the faraway land of Lebanon as a seventeen-year-old with fifty dollars in his pocket. Speaking only a few words of English, he enrolled first at Mt. Olive College in Mt. Olive,

North Carolina, the school from which he graduated with his Associates Degree in Business. He then enrolled in High Point University in North Carolina. Upon graduation, he took his innate business and entrepreneurial skills and set off to chase his horizon. Over time, Qubein became a sought-after consultant, speaker, and author of twenty-four books, rising to truly deserve the title of captain of his industry. From there, he began to heed Blackbeard's fifth principle.

From his book profits, Qubein created a scholarship fund for deserving students, a fund that eventually exceeded one million dollars. Founding a bank, buying a bread company, and serving on the board of directors of several major corporations were only stops on Qubein's great voyage, not its ultimate conquest. Finally, he made port again at High Point University when the former president retired and Qubein was tapped to take his place. He has held the helm of HPU for the last twelve years, and under his leadership, enrollment has increased by two hundred ten percent. While to my knowledge he has not taught anyone how to handle a musket properly, Qubein has been instrumental in bringing about deeper changes in the university, the contemporary equivalent of apprenticeship. Average SAT scores have risen by one hundred points and Qubein's campus has become student-focused, everything designed to lead to the success of the next generation, the future captains of the modern world.

As part of his leading efforts to aid the students as they prepare for their maiden voyages into the working world, Qubein has orchestrated the construction of ninety new buildings thus far, including a state-of-the-art healthcare facility to house the Congdon School of Health Sciences and the Fred Wilson School of Pharmacy. With his improvements costing nearly two point one billion dollars, Qubein again took responsibility for the thorough education of his numerous "apprentices" and has already helped raise three hundred million dollars to cover the costs.

Qubein's efforts are not limited to the visible. Perhaps his greatest achievement in the education of the next generation is less tangible even than the crew of the Dutchman. Qubein himself, never one to shirk his responsibilities as captain to his young crew, teaches a series of required courses for freshmen. In these courses, he arms his students with lessons on the importance of making a good impression, being remembered for the right reasons, recognizing that presenting ideas persuasively is a necessary precursor to achieving one's goals, and viewing college as more than just a place to collect information.

Additionally, under Qubein's guidance, his students embark on journeys to improve the world around them. Aboard Qubein's ship there is a culture of giving. While not required, students are encouraged to volunteer, and volunteer they do, with more than a hundred thousand hours served annually. In my journeys, I have come across HPU students and graduates who have made port to make positive change in as far flung places as the jungles of Guatemala, where their community service work touched hundreds of families each week.

A humble captain, Qubein brings global leaders to campus both as commencement speakers and as part of HPU's "Access to Innovators" series. Qubein's fleet of "apprentices" have been fortunate enough to hear from the likes of former Secretary of State, Chairman of the Joint Chiefs of Staff, and National Security Advisor General Colin Powell; former First Lady Laura Bush; U.S. Supreme Court Justice Clarence Thomas; Apple Co-Founder Steve Wozniak; sixty-sixth Secretary of State Condoleezza Rice; broadcast legend Tom Brokaw; former New York City Mayor Rudy Giuliani; Her Majesty Queen Noor of Jordan; NASA Astronaut Buzz Aldrin; Coca-Cola Company CEO Muhtar Kent; and bestselling authors Malcolm Gladwell, Wes Moore, and Seth Godin. Whatever course his students intend to chart, Qubein supplies them with the necessary tools, wisdom, and contacts to succeed.

A crew is only as strong as its weakest shot. Qubein is ensuring that every member of the crew of the next generation will have the target in view and shoot straight and true.

Unleashing the Inner Pyrate in Your World:

What two insights come to you regarding strengthening your efforts in mentoring as you read this Principle?

1.

2.

What do you need to make it happen in your world?

When will you do it?

Say What Ye Are Going to Do, Then Do It

VI

I have known other pyrate captains who have lost their reputations and were no longer feared b'cause they failed to carry out a threat… or a promise. They did not do what they said they would. I remember well Captain Stede Bonnet and his good ship Revenge. His crew voted him out when caution became his aim instead of his cannon. I warn ye not to do the same. Say it, do it. What be yer word worth?

Bonus Brethren Information

Pirates were known for being a thieving, god-forsaken bunch, but no matter the scoundrels the world may think them to be, if a pirate gave his word and swore an oath, he would stick to it. There are tales of pirates being forsworn, with a hand on the Bible (so that God be their judge) or on crossed hand axes or pistols, to properly sail and defend their ship to the very death. The pirate who failed to keep such an oath was considered traitorous to the ship and his shipmates, and would swiftly be thrown overboard, marooned, or killed.

In this way pirates were more free men than their fellow seafarers, such as merchant crew members or sailors in the Royal Navy. Those crews had no rights to speak of, whereas all who sailed under the Jolly Roger had a say on their ships. Captains were often elected by their crews, and every voyage began with the drawing up of articles to which every crew member was expected to affix his name and was then duty-bound to obey (1). Decades before the dawn of the French Revolution or even the Revolutionary War, documents bearing words worthy of gracing such declarations of democracy were written, signed, and followed faithfully aboard many a pirate ship.

Such articles not only dealt with liberty, fraternity, and equality, but also laid out a code of conduct to which every crew member was expected to adhere. They were likely to contain the following rules:

- Every man has a voice in all affairs.
- Every man has equal title to all fresh provisions and strong liquors seized.
- Captain and quartermaster receive two shares in a prize. Sailing master, boatswain, and gunner receive one-and-one-half shares. Other officers receive one-and-one-quarter shares, while sailors receive one share. If anyone loses a limb or becomes crippled in the common service, he receives a greater share.
- No gaming for money at cards or dice at sea.

- Lights and candles out before eight o'clock. Any drinking done after eight must be done on open decks.
- Every man must keep his gun, pistol, and cutlass clean and ready for service. If he does not, he shall be cut from his share and suffer further punishment as the captain sees fit.
- To desert a ship or abandon quarters in time of battle is punishable by death or marooning. The marooned man is given a bottle of water and some powder, a shot, and a pistol so that he may put himself out of his misery.
- If someone cheats the company of an article of value, he is punished by marooning.
- If a robbery takes place between two crewmen, the nose and ears of the guilty one will be split and he will be marooned.
- No women allowed on board. If any man carries a woman aboard in disguise, he is to be put to death.
- No striking another crew member on board. Every man's quarrel is to be settled on shore with sword and pistol. The quartermaster shall accompany the embattled pair to shore. The disputants are set back twenty paces. At the quartermaster's command, the two shall turn and fire immediately. If both miss, they shall take up their cutlasses.

Articles of this sort were at the heart of every functioning crew. For a ship to sail smoothly, everyone aboard must be true to his word.

::: APPLICATION :::

Marwin Company

Scattered across the Southeast, scores of happy consumers are customers of Jesse Davis's Marwin Company. Like Blackbeard, Davis is a veteran who was fresh out of uniform following his finishing of active duty (in this case serving in World War II) when he chose to chart his own course. Joining the post-war construction boom like Blackbeard joined the post-war Golden

Age of piracy, Davis named his new millwork company for his two sons, Marion (Mar) and Edwin (win), both of whom are still active in their father's company. Their primary product is not sophisticated: it is little more than a folding attic stairway system for new homes, but as the winds of change have blown across time, the company has expanded its offerings to include interior doors and pocket-door frames, in addition to energy-saving products.

The most boast-worthy output of Marwin Company, though, is the company's straightforward set of core values and the steadfast adherence to them by every member of the crew. As the pirates of old did at the start of every endeavor, Davis began his business venture by drawing up his own set of articles and posting the core values of the company for all to see, first in print and later on the home page of his website. While no one will be marooned for failing to adhere to Davis's articles, the clear core values set a precedent of honesty and dedication to producing a superior, dependable product and delivering it in a timely fashion. In order for the company to sail smoothly and compete successfully with imports, all employees must stay true to the core values. And stay true they do.

Relying on the skills of over a hundred duty-bound, article-abiding employees, the Marwin manufacturing system is fast-paced but safety-driven, just like a pirate vessel heading into conflict, utilizing the latest technology to shape the parts and pieces that comprise it. To keep the company afloat, every employee must stay on task and keep the core values in mind at all times. Thus the Marwin Company has expanded its distribution from its Columbia, South Carolina headquarters to include a Western Division headquartered in Mt. Pleasant, Texas. By incorporating employees in its corporate identity and expecting everyone, whatever their job, to hold themselves to the same core values, success flows easily to Marwin Company, riding on the waves of positivity that ripple outward from their loyal crew to their customers.

Unleashing the Inner Pyrate in Your World:

What could your company or organization learn from the establishment of and adherence to a very public set of core values?

1.

2.

What do you need to make it happen in your world?

When will you do it?

VII

All Good Plans Include Yer Shipmates

Whilst it is true that many pyrate captains are elected by their crews to lead independently, it be good to include yer mates in plans. The captain, a'course, has the final say, but a wise one keeps his crew informed. When preparing for a cruize, call a counsel of War. Know where ye be headed, and share it.

Then there shall be times when ye, as captain, make the decision on yer own. This May (1718), the Queen Anne's Revenge saw herself off of the shores of Charles Towne. The towne was not well armed, and soe ripe for ravaging and me crew was in dire need of certain supplies from on shore.

Heeding me crew's needs, I directed the Queen Anne's Revenge toward Charles Towne. We hove to outside the harbour so that our ships met vessels coming and going. We then captured an important citizen, Samuel Wragg. We held him ransom for me demands. At that time the crew needed medicine to address a variety of ills – certain crew members spent too many a night cracking Jenny's teacup whilst ashore and were paying the price twice. Our surgeon was out of medicine. Charles Towne has it in abundance. Fair exchange: a chest of medicine fer a leading citizen.

A'course, o'er the six days we were waiting fer the ransom we intercepted nine ships and removed a variety of goods from their cargo holds. And still not a shot was fired.

Sometimes there shall be profitable returns, sometimes not soe profitable. The highest value lay in the meeting of me crew's needs.

Bonus Brethren Information

Pirates created their own community. A captain took a motley bunch of men, some out-of-work veterans of the sea, others adventure seekers, and still others looking to escape authorities, and transformed them into a crew. Pirating was what might now be called a great exercise in team building.

Once this newly-formed crew stepped aboard their new home, ties to their former lives were severed like the lines mooring their ship to the docks. Disciplines once imposed by the church, family, and local authorities were lost astern and a new social order, formed by these brethren, took their place.

Included in this social order was the revolutionary concept of workers' compensation. Exact amounts varied from ship to ship, at times not even listed in the articles of the vessel, but the standard among the Brethren of the Coast was to compensate for wounds somewhat as follows:

- Loss of an eye earned one hundred pieces of eight
- Loss of a right arm entitled a pirate to two hundred
- Loss of a left arm called for five hundred
- Loss of a finger was settled with one hundred
- Loss of a leg left a man with four hundred (1)

(*As of the writing of this book, silver was being traded in the US for 24.06 an oz. Each piece of eight was equal to 1/8 of a dollar*).

::: APPLICATION :::

Zappos

Big-name companies like Google, SAP, and Microsoft have clearly heeded the pirates' precedent of treating workers fairly and thereby ensuring employee retention, offering huge perks for whoever comes aboard including flexible hours, casual dress codes, complimentary restaurant-quality food supplied on site, and fun activities to keep ideas and energy flowing more freely than the Sound. How can smaller companies adhere to this age-old but still revolutionary principle of treating employees well and maintaining healthy work environments?

The key to that secret might have been long buried with its pirating pioneers, but Tony Hseish (pronounced "Shey"), founder of Zappos, seems to have discovered it. Zappos, short for the Spanish word for shoes, zapatos, is devoted first and foremost to its crew. The hiring and training process can take eighty or so days as Zappos leaders painstakingly take new recruits through four weeks of orientation alone to ensure that their new shipmates are steady on their sea legs before sending them off to their new tasks.

The crew of Zappos is far from motley, with Hseish deliberately seeking out those who see their new work opportunity as more of a calling than a job. Once on board and trained, employees are treated to full medical insurance coverage, free food and snacks, and a generally positive atmosphere. Most employees' cubicles are decorated to express their personalities, including the cubicle of their captain. While most captains of industry keep millions of dollars of profits for themselves, Hseish insists his salary remain just thirty-seven thousand dollars a year (a wage he can afford to request after selling his former business for thirty million dollars when he was a mere twenty-four years old). His low salary allows the company to afford its unique offer: without needing to lose a limb, employees can opt to quit and go to work elsewhere and receive a payment of two to three thousand dollars in severance.

This understanding of the importance of taking great care of one's crew extends beyond Hseish's employees. Like a good commodore, Hseish sees beyond those aboard his own ship to the others who help keep his company afloat: his customers. Zappos employees are taught the importance of great customer service along with the rest of the core values of the company. Under the articles of Zappos, as posted on the company's website, employees must:

- Deliver "wow" through service
- Embrace and drive change; create fun "and a little weirdness"
- Remain adventurous, creative, and open-minded
- Pursue learning and growth
- Build honest relationships through communication
- Build a positive team and family spirit
- Do more with less
- Stay passionate and determined
- Stay humble (2)

Though these articles may be a far cry from the contents of those aboard a pirate vessel, the outcome is strikingly similar. Everyone engaged with Zappos, crew and customers alike, is a valued part of the company and is treated as such.

Zappos employees need not sever ties with the outside world. In fact, the company's telephone policy is unique in that its call time is limitless. Employees are encouraged not to cut off or rush a customer for the sake of short-term efficiency and actually can help callers for hours on end, until their needs are met, going so far as to searching up to three competitors for an out-of-stock item and directing customers there. One legendary customer call lasted five hours, the Zappos crew member remaining dutifully on the line to hear and help with all of the customer's needs. Hseish is so concerned with the care of his extended customer "crew" that over one-third of the company's employees – five hundred out of fourteen hundred workers – are members of the Customer Loyalty Team whose sole goal is to provide exemplary customer service.

Fostering a positive environment and loyal crew and consumer base, Zappos ships a hundred thousand units daily and was deemed worthy of joining Amazon's fleet, purchased by them in 2009 for one point three billion dollars. All because at Zappos, the best decisions are those made with and for the crew.

Unleashing the Inner Pyrate in Your World:

How can you include your own crew in your plans for the benefit of your company?

1.

2.

What do you need to make it happen in your world?

When will you do it?

Be the Captain

VIII

Set the standard and live by it, good or ill. If ye wish to give no quarter, then do soe. Hesitation will cost ye yer hard fought-fer reputation, and perhaps e'en yer life. Having principles allows ye to do what needs be done to accomplish yer mission. Let nothing and no one stand in yer way. Ye be in charge. Ye be responsible fer the welfare of yer crew.

Good captains are out in the Sea air, keeping the helmsmen on course. Ye set it. Feel the heat off the Tropics and the air that comes from jist off shore or the spray in a storm. The greatest is the thrill of the chase. Yer crew shall look to ye fer inspiration. Ye canna do that inside the comfort of yer cabin, e'en with a good bottle of port or rum.

Bonus Brethren Information

Every soul aboard a ship was duty-bound to fulfill his role, the captain being no exception. Elected by their crews with each man casting one vote, captains were at times known to call councils to determine the route of their ship's next cruise, but the moment their ship entered the fray, the captain's word alone was what mattered. A good captain led by example, unhesitatingly fighting at the front of his crew, first over the gunwale.

Among these seafaring thieves, though, there were a few captains without honor. Captain Edward Low was renowned for his brutality with friend and foe alike, murdering for good humor or, as he once did, over something a small as a punch bowl (1).

In his time at the helm, Blackbeard came across some who did not deserve the mantle of captaincy. One such man was Stede Bonnet, a gentleman merchant who traded his legal life for the more thrilling one of piracy. After purchasing his own vessel and assembling his crew, Bonnet fell under the influence of Blackbeard and his crew. The more seasoned pirate captain hoped to shape the novice into a capable captain and took Bonnet aboard the Queen Anne's Revenge to mentor him. But even legends as great as Blackbeard have their failures. Once left again to his own devices after training under Blackbeard, Bonnet became a cruel captain, abusing his crew and killing many of those he captured. When his fall became inevitable, he announced his plan to blow up his ship rather than surrender. His crew, their lack of loyalty a reflection of Bonnet's poor leadership, overruled their former captain and gave themselves up instead.

Bonnet's poor captaincy ended with a hempen jig, as did that of his fellow failure of a captain, Charles Vane. Reputed to be one of the cruelest pirate captains in the seven seas, Vane murdered a popular crew member and swiftly found himself voted out as captain, marooned at Port Royal, Jamaica, and even robbed of the opportunity to use his mercy pistol shot by authorities who swiftly hanged him by the neck.

When a ship found itself in the hands of an incapable captain, others had to step up and take command before the scurvy seadog scuttled their ship with his poor leadership skills. Wild and colorful Captain "Calico Jack" Rackham inadvertently found a true leader for his ship when he brought aboard Anne Bonny and her cross-dressing friend, Mary Reed. Quite taken by the scandalously-reputed Bonny, Rackham attempted to persuade her husband, former pirate Jack Bonny, to grant her an annulment, but to no avail. Nonetheless, when Rackham's crew stole the twelve-ton, six-gun sloop, the William, and set sail from its Nassau port, Bonny and Reed were among them. Over the course of the next two months, Calico Jack seemed competent, his crew growing along with his name as he picked up and plundered small vessels and generally made life interesting for those unfortunate enough to attempt to ship goods in and out of Nassau. His infamy grew to the point that Wood Rogers, the new Royal Governor of the island, hired privateers to seek out and capture the William.

Calico Jack entered a game of cat and mouse with the privateers, a game during which a good captain would never let down his guard. Calico Jack proved himself a poor captain indeed when he allowed his crew to grow rowdy and drunk, partying through the night until their fun was interrupted by the sudden boarding of their ship by the pursuing privateer's crew. It was then that Bonny and Reed earned their fame without ever being formally given the title of captain or even quartermaster. (The role Blackbeard likely played aboard Hornigold's ship, the quartermaster is the representative of the crew to the captain and peacemaker and punisher of the crew.) The two "unlucky" women aboard called the crew to stations and fought fiercely despite being grossly outnumbered. Surrounded by enemies and a drunken crew, the two brave women at last were forced to surrender.

Back on shore, Bonny and Reed were tried and condemned as pirates along with the rest of the crew, but were spared their lives as both were with child. Visiting Calico Jack in prison for the last time before his execution, Reed told the failed, felled captain, "I'm sorry to see you here, but if you had fought like a man, you need not be hanged like a dog" (2). Harsh parting words from one of the true captains of his ship.

::: APPLICATION :::

Kraft Group

When one is said to be a captain in one's field, it is generally not meant as literally as Robert K. Kraft means it. Chairman and CEO of Kraft Group, a diversified holding company, Kraft takes after Blackbeard in the vastness of his influence. Like Blackbeard who, at the height of his influence, had up to five vessels in his flotilla, Kraft is truly due the title of commodore, each of his ships captained by a quartermaster he appoints. Kraft himself remains firmly at the top of a clear and communicative chain of command. Among Kraft's fleet are the New England Patriots, which he bought in 1994 to fulfill a lifelong dream as a diehard fan (and season ticket holder since 1971).

As an avid supporter of the team, Kraft's priority was leading his players to victory. The key to that victory, Kraft understood, was ensuring that he had the most capable captains at the helm of his team, and he surrounded himself with strong leaders. When Bill Purcells retired from the Patriots, skeptics believed the players were destined to feed the fish. Earlier, in a move as surprising to some as finding two women in control of a pirate ship, Kraft hired Bill Belichick, a recently fired head coach who had had mixed success in Cleveland. Had Commodore Kraft lost his wits?

Initially, Belichick was brought on as a quartermaster, a secondary coach, but after the integral role he played in the team's Super Bowl win and Purcells's retirement, Kraft gave him full captaincy of the Patriots, promoting Belichick to head coach. Kraft, ignoring the abounding scuttlebutt in the media that the Patriots were doomed to sink to the bottom, trusted the gut feeling he couldn't credit to Harvard Business School.

In Super Bowl LI, it appeared the skeptics were to be proven right and a storm was brewing to bring the Patriots down to Davy Jones. Losing twenty-one to three to the Atlanta Falcons at halftime, Belichick called for all hands on deck. Assembling his team, Belichick delivered no expletive-filled, violent halftime speech. He left no smashed chairs or cracked chalkboard in his wake, nor did his eloquent speech gush forth like a powerful jetstream. Instead, he splashed his crew with the quick reminder of the duty to which they all were bound, the duty he, in doing so, upheld. "Do your job." Changes were made to the game plan and the team was sent out to play.

Leaving the distractions of the season, including the infamy and shame of "Inflate-Gate," on the shores of their locker room, Belichick led his team over the gunwale into the second half of the game. And for the second of half of Super Bowl LI, all fifty-three members of the team followed their captain's, their coach's, example and did their jobs, making history by coming back and winning the game, led by their master gunner, quarterback Tom Brady. After a year of adversity, Belichick proved that a true captain has no need of long speeches or fancy words. His example should be enough to lead his crew, and the proof is in their victories.

And it all flows back to their commodore. Kraft saw the potential for greatness in Belichick and took him aboard to become the strong captain the team needed him to be. Known for taking risks, Kraft encouraged the graduating class of Yeshiva University in New York to follow his lead in his 2016 commencement speech. Even before the rest of the world saw the treasure he had found in trusting captain Belichick to lead the Patriots to a Super Bowl win, Kraft dared the graduates to dream and to be the first over the gunwale.

Unleashing the Inner Pyrate in Your World:

What knowledge have you gained about leadership from the simple style of Commodore Kraft and his Captain Belichick?

1.

2.

What do you need to make it happen in your world?

When will you do it?

Be Not Predictable In All Yer Matters

Ye draw close to the vessel ye be pursuing. Guns drawn. Cannon primed. The other captain is already making his peace with God whilst desperately throwing cargo overboard to gain speed. Ye have outmaneuvered him or drived him aground. What have ye done in the past that he shall expect ye to do? Do the opposite. Keep yer enemies and targets guessing, do the unexpected, take the risk, go fer the prize.

Bonus Brethren Information

Blackbeard was not the only unpredictable pirate to sail the seven seas during the Golden Age. Captain Jean Lafitte made his name and fortune by quietly bringing his ship close to its targeted vessel under the cover of night. Catching the targeted ship's night watch snoozing or daydreaming, Lafitte and his crew would board and take control of the ship without so much as a whimper.

In another surprising twist, Lafitte offered to help defend Louisiana during the War of 1812 and benefited the country rather than just his own crew by playing a pivotal role in the tide-turning Battle of New Orleans. Ultimately, Lafitte profited personally from his bold move, receiving a pardon from President James Madison (1).

Even the not-always-reliable Calico Jack at times adhered to Blackbeard's principle of unpredictability. Preparing to set sail from their hideaway, Calico Jack and his crew found themselves face to face with a Spanish man-of-war. Fleeing back to the safer, shallow waters to hide, Calico Jack made the quick and daring decision to abandon ship, instead boarding and capturing the Spanish ship under the cover of night. When the Spanish fired upon Calico Jack's ship and sought out what they thought to be a pirate vessel brimming with booty, they were met with nothing but an empty hull (2). Calico Jack and his crew lived to tell the tale and reap their rewards.

::: APPLICATION :::

Dr. Pearse Lyons

When the first Irishman to earn a formal degree from the British School of Malting and Brewing – a descendant of five generations of barrel makers – arrived on the shores of the United States, one would have expected him to arm himself with his Master's in Brewing and PhD in yeast fermentation and join the crew of a major brewery or distillery. Dr. Pearse Lyons, however, is anything but predictable.

Lyons began his maiden voyage in the United States by

founding an animal-feed business in 1980 with ten thousand dollars in capital. Like the enterprising, pioneering pirates of old, Lyons revolutionized his new field through the introduction of natural ingredients to feed. To keep his new business afloat, Lyons created thirty-five hundred jobs around the globe and raked in revenues in excess of one billion dollars.

One would then think that he would batten down the hatches and enjoy the smooth sailing of his successful business, but Lyons was not one to shy away from surprising adventures. Already one of the top ten players in the international animal-feed industry, Lyons set out to capture the brewery world, returning unexpectedly to his original passion for spirits. In a move that would make one of Hollywood's rowdy, rum-soaked pirates weep, Lyons founded a brewery in Lexington, Kentucky, the heart of bourbon territory.

Never one to settle into the boat trails of those before him, Lyons would not be satisfied producing just another craft beer; instead, he took the standard IPA and placed it in recycled bourbon barrels (available in abundance in the Commonwealth) for six weeks. The result is a craft beer with a new twist and a regional influence, a potent and tasty product he aptly christened Kentucky Bourbon Barrel Ale. Legend has it that those who have tried to stray from the type of trailblazing exemplified by Blackbeard and Lyons, and simply stealing Lyons's secret, have failed to successfully mimic his beer, even when Lyons went so far as to give them the recipe. Kentucky Bourbon Barrel Ale remains at the forefront of the fleet of craft beers in the country and is now being distributed in twenty-five states.

Borrowing from Blackbeard's other principle of apprenticeship, Lyons refused to be satisfied remaining calmly in the port of his successful brewery business, and instead turned to education. Like a true leader, he saw a need and did the unexpected. With the Commonwealth accounting for ninety-five percent of the world's bourbon production, Lyons was flabbergasted by the fact that there was no program in place to educate future brewers not only from the production side of the industry, but the business side as well (3).

Veering his ship yet again into uncharted waters, Lyons began a casual conversation with Western Kentucky University's (WKU) President Gary Ransdell about creating a brewing and distilling academy on campus and left it at that. Dr. Ransdell and his leadership team responded within a week, floating the idea of building a brewery on campus in WKU's Center for Research and Development.

A crew of Alltech's Lexington Brewing and Distilling Co.'s professionals are now working with WKU in the school's new program in Brewing and Distilling Arts and Science. Those students whose compasses point toward the new program find themselves working in a real craft brewery. And so, by again making the unexpected move and not simply having students pretend to brew beer in a lab, Lyons ensured that students and company profit. Students who set off on their own after graduation find themselves far from unprepared for their maiden voyages, carrying with them an understanding of the big picture and actual hands-on experience that help them find real jobs – should they even choose to do what is expected, that is.

Unleashing the Inner Pyrate in Your World:

What uncharted waters, rich with new niches and needs, do you see in your world and how can you veer your career's course into them to take advantage of unexpected opportunities?

1.

2.

What do you need to make it happen in your world?

When will you do it?

Fear Not -
Show Yer True Colours

Make sure yer flagg represents who ye be as a captain. Any old scallywag can fly the Jolly Roger, but those who fix yer center mast in their telescope shall find yer flagg and see in it all the promises ye have become known fer. Fear arriving early on the deck o' the other ship clears an easy path for ye to board 'em.

The ship ye be approaching needs to see ye on the stern and know by the flagg ye be flying and yer presence on deck that ye and yer crew shall win the day.

Mind ye, there also be captains that draw their prey in closer fer the kill by flying a friendly flagg. Why continue to fight or run?

Bonus Brethren Information

Pirates of the tricky sort mentioned by Blackbeard included the ruthless Edward Low, who would fly the Spanish flag long enough to draw an unsuspecting ship to its doom, then run up the black flag when it was too late for his prey to escape (1). Charles Vane, though known to primarily fly black colors, was not above raising a French flag when it suited his purposes, and Samuel Bellamy would affix the British King's ensign and pennant to the mast of his Whydah in order to attack Irish vessels. Bartholomew Roberts went a step further, readying himself for different strategies by keeping an English ensign, a Dutch pennant, and a black flag (2).

Flags were not always used to fool foes. They have been used for communication between men-of-war for centuries. The concept was expanded by Dutch Admiral Michiel de Ruyter, resulting in his success against the British fleet. Among pirate vessels, ships would communicate with other ships by hoisting a green silk flag depicting a yellow male figure blowing a trumpet to call a council (3). This derived from the use of a speaking trumpet to communicate between ships within shouting distance (4). Pirates also affixed a red flag to the mizzen peak in place of their traditional flags in order to signal that there was no quarter given or taken (5).

::: APPLICATION :::

Anders Lewendal Construction

Colors remain central to communication at sea to this day. The stern of a ship will bear the flag of the country to which it is registered, whereas the mizzen will often bear the flag of the country in which a vessel is sailing to signal respect and deference to the country's laws. On land, though, one typically does not see companies flying their flags on their trucks and buildings. Instead, flags have found a new form in slogans and mission statements, as exemplified by Anders Lewendal Construction. In place of a trumpet or a red banner, their website bears their motto "If you can dream it, we can build it" (6). Simple, bold, and upheld steadfastly by Lewendal and his crew since 1991. To Anders Lewendal, his wife, Marilyn de Kleer, and their son Jack, the motto is more than just a phrase. It is what they do. It is who they are. It is a flag faithful to the principles of Blackbeard.

Their adventure beginning long before the course to building a company was clear, the Lewendal-de Kleer family travelled through the United States, camping where they could. Along their journey, they fell in love with Bozeman, Montana, weighed anchor, and the rest is history. As their flag boasts, they have become builders of homes, spec and custom – builders with a mission, a purpose. Initially, they took up the flag of the "green" movement (one that now bears the title of "sustainable") and unwaveringly built environmentally sustainable houses through the use of recycled building materials, renewable energy sources like solar panels, and efficient designs. By staying true to that which their green flag represented, the Lewendals ensure that both their company and their customers profit, since the new homeowners save a great deal of money on heating and energy over time due to the careful insulation of the houses.

Never abandoning their primary flag, their motto of making dreams come true, the Lewendals made another decision, one that would help them navigate the most recent housing downturn. Anders yearned to show his true colors, beyond green, and dared to build a single-family home using only materials made in the United States. The idea made waves and Lewendal's project was featured on ABC television, garnering unprecedented publicity for a small single-family builder.

Last I heard from the Lewendals, they were again expanding their horizons by also building spec homes as well as custom houses and townhouses, all while still building sustainable housing with an "All-American Home" option (by which customers can opt to weigh anchor in a house built entirely with products made in the United States).

Lewendal and his company are not flying false flags to draw in their targets. They understand the impact of housing on the environment and American economy and dutifully do their research to ensure that they truly represent the multiple flags they raise. For his sustainable homes, Lewendal adds extra, enticing features behind and beneath the walls. His building style is inspired by his belief that a decision needs to be made during the planning process, not skimping in the short term by making the house so tight that it generates moisture issues and money loss down the road. His loyalty to his flag has kept him aloft as well. The All-American Home he built in 2011 has all of the sustainable features, plus a reasonable ROI (return on investment) for the owners, all with a HERS (Home Energy Rating System) of less than forty. In other words, this home has reduced the need for energy by sixty percent when compared with other homes. Homes built beneath the flag of Anders Lewendal Construction will last several generations with minimal increase in cost to building the home.

His old green flag has not weighed Lewendal down on his new course toward building with only products produced in the U.S. Along this mapless voyage, Lewendal and his company discovered Maze Nails, made in the U.S. and used in a variety of tasks involved in construction. While the American-made nails cost a bit more than those shipped from offshore, the former did not jam the workers' nail guns, unlike those produced by their foreign competitors. Offshore nails jammed nail guns so frequently that they caused costly delays as the crew had to take time to remove and replace the faulty product. It seemed that American-made Maze Nails were as valuable as dry powder aboard a pirate ship.

Unsatisfied with the attainable goal of tightening and transforming his own ship by switching to American-made materials, Anders aims to get residential builders to reallocate a mere five percent of their construction spending to U.S.-produced products, the predicted result being a fourteen-billion-dollar bounty for the U.S. economy, a boon that will ripple out in the form of a score of potentially well-paying jobs. Anders, sailing steadily under his flags of sustainability, American-made products, and his ever-true motto, is setting course to change the world.

Unleashing the Inner Pyrate in Your World:

This principle features a small business that has made the decision to lead an industry. What concepts do you have that would bring you to the helm of your business segment or cause as you steer your industry in a new direction?

1.

2.

What do you need to make it happen in your world?

When will you do it?

Eyes on the Horizon - Is it the Enemy or an Opportunity?

XI

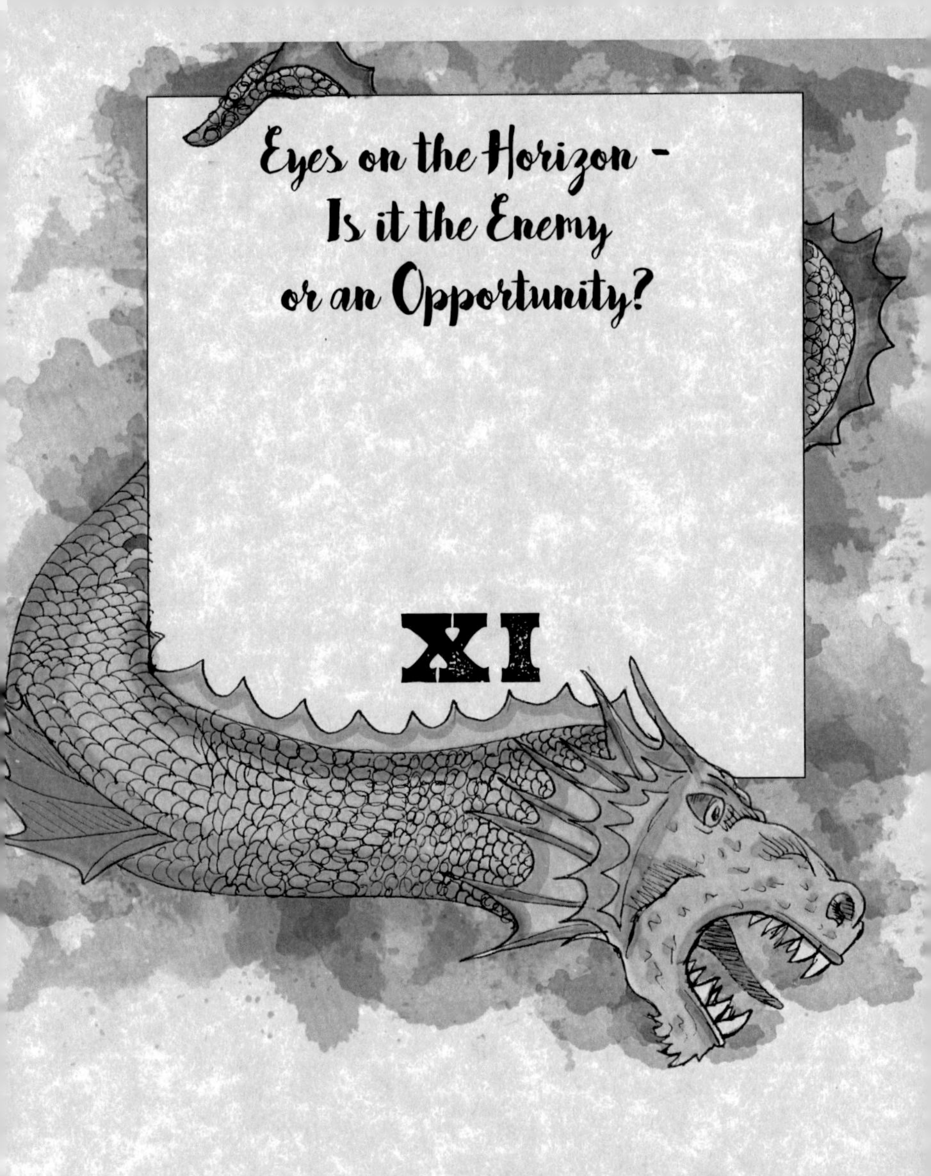

Be on the watch: whether in port or at Sea, ye must have lookers-out minding the light at the masthead for what lies just over the horizon. What does the mainmast say to 'em? What flagg be they flying? What does that information tell yer crew about the type of ship, say, or about the crew and cargo?

Bonus Brethren Information

The tallest point on sailing vessels in Blackbeard's day, the mainmast, also contained a place for a lookout (known as the crow's nest). Manned from dawn 'til dusk, as Blackbeard advised, the crew member stationed in the crow's nest was constantly on the lookout for other ships. The more seasoned seamen could often identify other ships at a distance simply by their silhouette, and they were able to warn their shipmates of approaching men-of-war, merchantmen, or perhaps other pirates. The job came with a special incentive: there was an extra share of the booty in store for the pirate who spotted the vessel, should it prove to be a prize.

Ships were not the only things lurking just beyond the horizon. The area of the Caribbean and much of the East Coast of what would become America was often plagued with storms that came suddenly upon unsuspecting ships, leaving great damage and pain in their wake. Given some warning from a lookout with a sharp, sober eye, a crew could batten down the hatches and sail into the storm rather than being struck sideways or simply swept below the gigantic waves whipped up by the fierce winds.

Failure to catch the storms before they struck inevitably ended in disaster, as Captain Samuel Bellamy and his crew learned shortly before going down to meet Davy Jones. Bellamy's ship, the Whydah, was caught up by a Nor'easter while sailing off the coast of Boston on April 26, 1717. Despite the heroic efforts of the pirate crew and their captain, the Whydah ran aground near Cape Cod, though not before the gale swept Bellamy and much of his crew into the raging seas and pulled them down to the Locker. Only two members of the crew survived on the island whereupon their ship had been grounded, and they soon joined their shipmates after their rescuers turned them in to the authorities to be tried and hanged.

::: APPLICATION :::

MarketGraphics / The Market Edge

In the turbulent waters of today's economy, particularly in the choppy seas of the housing industry, one must keep a weather eye on the horizon. Even experts, blinded by the spray of the storm, struggle to navigate the housing economy. Landlocked in Tennessee, two companies have surfaced to serve as guides through these stormy seas, dedicating themselves to mastering the art of seeing what lies on the horizon.

Just south of Nashville lies a crow's nest in the form of MarketGraphics Research Group Inc.'s headquarters. Founded by Edsel Charles in 1988, MarketGraphics provides comprehensive new home and residential development research and forecasting data, serving a diverse clientele. As it has from day one, MarketGraphics offers a highly personalized service aimed at providing structure to the strategic planning efforts of its clients so that they may chart their next course safely and smartly. Utilizing its market data, the MarketGraphics crew helps clients play to their strengths as they navigate the housing and development market. Among its armada of customers are builders, developers, bankers, and companies that serve to supply accurate information on current trends in new construction. This fleet of consumers is scattered across the country; MarketGraphics serves twenty-one markets across eighteen states.

Building its contemporary crow's nest with the aid of modern technology, MarketGraphics gathers material from the captains of various communities and industries, thus amassing a treasure trove of data that is on-target as to what has been built and what is being built. Organized like a well-run ship by location and price, MarketGraphics information also includes available lots, along with their stages of development. Like the pirates of old, MarketGraphics maps out its findings in charts that provide an array of priceless information for those in need of help seeing what lies on their horizons.

Edsel Charles, captain of this great enterprise, is a worthy lookout. Now considered by many captains of the industry as a reliable voice regarding the direction of the once-unchartable housing market in the United States, Charles began his career as a humble brick mason in his home state of Wisconsin. Along his voyage to the top of the industry, Charles amassed a wealth of knowledge and experience as a builder, developer, and realtor, and acquainted himself with every aspect of his field like a powder monkey making his way through the ranks to captaincy. Now a much-beloved speaker, endeared by his Midwestern accent and enlightening Power Points, his voice was once unheeded when his sharp eyes spotted the looming housing crash and predicted it to the day years in advance (1). Having now proven his remarkable ability to predict a desolating storm, Charles continues to keep a weather eye on the horizon, his company adhering to its gale-tested methods.

At the crow's nest of MarketGraphics, lookouts must watch for shifts in the specific markets they serve and have versatile reports to adapt to changes and shifts, allowing clients on deck to have clarity as to which issues are most pertinent to address. They work closely with their clients, establishing fundamental market identifiers as benchmarks for judging the strength or weakness of a market. When descending from their lookout post to speak with customers, MarketGraphics crew members carefully tailor their presentations to meet the specific needs of each client within a market – rather than foggy predictions made haphazardly en masse to maximize pricing and get the most monetarily out of each situation – resulting in loyal, long-term relationships.

For those who wish to keep a greater distance from the crow's nest but still needing information on what lurks on the housing industry's horizon, Dale Adkins holds the treasure. (2) After seven years as a humble banker working with builders and developers, Adkins saw his entrepreneurial future just over the horizon. In 2001, he mapped out a new course for himself to provide accurate housing start information to the industry in a variety of markets. And so, from the steady stream of Adkins's obscure but informative life as a banker, The Market Edge sprang forth as a guide on the wide and dangerous waters of the housing industry.

Unlike MarketGraphics, The Market Edge sends information down from the crow's nest to a website where those seeking information can unearth a series of free reports available for download. Aiming to provide the suppliers and vendors from the housing industry, who wait on the decks below them, with accurate housing start information, The Market Edge gathers information weekly. It provides its readers with detailed reports that include even the GPS coordinates for sale and delivery of goods and services. The Market Edge has also broadened its horizons by providing reports on the status of commercial construction as well.

Research for these reports is conducted by actually making the voyages to Code offices, rather than merely compiling housing start numbers. Throughout 2015, The Market Edge's horizons included two hundred thirty-eight Code offices, representing one hundred ten counties, from which the company's lookout compiled data. In total, The Market Edge serves eighteen markets in seven states.

Setting the example with his keen eye, Akins is also watching the horizons for future generations. A long-time volunteer with Big Brothers and Big Sisters, Akins has served both as a matched mentor and as a board member. For his dedication to this worthy cause, he was among those recognized with the National Hero Medallion. Akins continues to use his skills as a lookout to help children chart better courses for their lives.

Though their crow's nests take different shapes, both MarketGraphics and The Market Edge have mastered the art of keeping a weather eye on the horizon. Lookouts at MarketGraphics use detailed statistics gathered quarterly to help builders and developers determine where and what they should be building. Those who sit atop the mainmast at The Market Edge compile information on a weekly basis and pass it along to the myriad of crews who supply goods and services to the building industry. Thanks to these two loyal lookouts, the countless crews engaged in the housing industry can hope to stay afloat, gifted with a clearer view of what lies just beyond their horizons.

Unleashing the Inner Pyrate in Your World:

How does your company or organization measure or forecast what is headed your way? How can you apply this principle to ensure your safe passage through stormy seas?

1.

2.

What do you need to make it happen in your world?

When will you do it?

Keep Yer Powder Dry

XII

No sense going into a fight if yer cannon and shot stay on yer ship. Keep yer stores of gunpowder dry and ready fer battle. A good barrel maker and carpenter is a valuable asset, keeping his trade tight and water out. Make sure that yer barrels of gunpowder are always safe and easy to access in case of an unexpected fray.

Bonus Brethren Information

When signing the articles of his ship, each pirate took an oath to take care of his own equipment, be it pistols, knives, cutlasses, or other weaponry. Part of their specific roles as members of the crew was to lend a hand in keeping rope in great shape since is could not be replaced at sea. When their captain found a safe place to careen the vessel, most of the crew pitched in and helped clean off the accumulated sea life that had affixed itself to the bottom of the ship.

Barrels were the responsibility of the carpenter, who would also make sure that cracks and split lumber on the vessel were properly addressed. The boatswain took care of the sails and masts while gun crews, as one might expect, maintained the ship's guns. With its weapons cleaned and oiled and ready for action, and its barrels of powder safe and secure, a pirate ship was only as good as its equipment.

::: APPLICATION :::

Cyber-Security

In today's business world, dry and safe gunpowder may not be the most important of assets. That by no means renders Blackbeard's advice obsolete. The "barrels" of businesses in the twenty-first century are filled with financial information, information for getting a message to market, directions for personnel, or the contact information of customers and members both current and prospective. The importance of keeping this information confidential varies according to its application. For instance, a personnel manual with guidelines, directives, and policies is important only to those who are part of the company unless it contains proprietary knowledge. Of great or small value, information has become the powder of the contemporary age, and it is vital for companies of all sorts to keep it safe and ready for use.

Some of the most priceless powders a company can store and use are research and development information and secret formulae. Coca Cola has managed to protect its powerful powder for decades, carefully keeping its secret soda recipe locked away tighter than a treasure chest in chains. Apple and Samsung are continuously replacing their barrels of powder, cautiously containing and insulating the details of the product release they have waiting just beyond the horizon so that their close competitors cannot use the information as their own ammunition. Tesla, too, has invaluable powder that they keep dry in the form of their yet-unexposed, revolutionary research into battery technology in a world where more and more green flags are being raised.

It is key to follow in the boat trails of this flotilla of successful companies. Companies must keep market research as accurate as possible to ensure that their unique message reaches as many people as possible, but such information should not be accidentally fired from a company's cannon. All hands must beware the dampening quality of leaked information and refrain from connecting personal computers or laptops to the web.

Nonprofits need to heed Blackbeard's warning as well. They, too, have precious powder in their holds, powder that takes the form of minutes from Board of Directors' meetings, financial information, plans for the future, and donor lists. While transparency is considered positive in the current cultural environment, a nonprofit must control the flow of information rather than allowing an outside party to board them and decide what should be shared and when.

For- and not-for-profit businesses today may not face the cannons of their competitors, but they certainly have adversaries aiming to sabotage their work for their own gain – not to mention malicious hackers who act out of sheer malice. And so the carpenters of the twenty-first century have emerged in the form of cyber-sleuths who work to keep the barrels of various companies watertight and safe. One such carpenter is Steve Hunt, an expert in the field of cyber-security (1). He graciously shared with me several key elements to keep a black spot from forming on a company.

First, consider the risks. People understand that their physical property may be stolen, and so they watch the horizon for crow's nests of thieves monitoring their property and life patterns. The crow's nests of cyber stalkers are harder to spot but no less real. Hackers have developed electronic robots, Hunt explained, introducing me to the industry jargon for them: "bots" or "bot-nets." These bots set out on recon missions by the millions, seeking out weaknesses in systems. When weaknesses are discovered, another, specialized bot is dispatched to check the strength of the firewall standing guard and the type of information being protected by the potentially permeable panelling of the technological barrel. If the information is deemed worthy of the battle, another bot, this one with skills in defeating firewalls, is sent to widen the cracks in the barrel and accumulate information contained therein. Often the violated company or organization will have no idea that its vessel has been boarded, nor which information has been compromised.

If a company or organization has eyes sharp enough to see that its powder has been sabotaged, Hunt suggests that its management call a cyber-security firm and ask for an Incident Response Team (IRT). These savvy crews discover how the firewall was breached, which information was taken, and perhaps even an evidence trail to follow in order to uncover who perpetrated the penetration.

Best, however, is to diligently keep your powder dry and safe, preventing a breach in the first place. Need companies return to the ways of pirates, scrawling their treasured information by hand on parchment and locking it away in a physical chest? Not necessarily, according to Hunt. Precious powder can be kept on a computer, but only one that has no access to or from the outside world even through networking with computers within a corporate system.

Furthermore, he encourages captains of companies to take proactive action and bring in a crew of computational carpenters, an IRT, as a precaution to prevent breaches. The crew will determine whether there are any weaknesses in the security of the company or organization. Companies such as Hunt Business Intelligence offer modern-day privateering of sorts, hacking legally and beneficently in order to find flaws in a system. A privateer hacker may operate clandestinely, known only to one member of the firm under examination, in order to do accurate "penetration testing."

Like privateers, these professionals live on the edge of lawfulness. Before they get started, they ask their contact in the company's crew how many rules they are cleared to break. While there are a variety of approaches that inspire different answers to that question, the cyber-security carpenters are often allowed to be as hands-on as need be. They could, for instance, swipe an employee badge, jimmy a door, or log on through a fake user account to get inside restricted areas to take photos, insert "smart sticks" into key computers, and generally gather as huge a haul of information as possible. To do so, they may present themselves in the guise of employees or sit in areas where crew members break or eat lunch and thus commit a form of espionage older than the legends of the pirates: just listening.

Who are the enemies posing such a threat that captains of companies need to call in carpenters to take such extreme measures?

There are a variety of hackers at several levels sailing into the worlds of for- and not-for-profit businesses. If WikiLeaks has a company in its crosshairs, that company had better hope it has a capable carpenter or make its peace with God. A favorite form of powder for WikiLeaks is Personally Identifiable Information (PII). With powder stolen from the cracked barrels of an armada of ships, WikiLeaks has long played a role in business and of late has begun to navigate the treacherous waters of politics, waters in which the Russians have already been sailing for ages.

Recently the Russians' love of the data-theft game and their presumed prowess in the art of obtaining information for financial gain and to compromise others' powder has grown to great infamy. The Chinese, on the other hand, are known for targeting intellectual property, i.e. trade secrets. I have personally witnessed numerous powder thefts by Chinese companies.

In an earlier day, when the worldwide web was not yet an arena for espionage, I was a part of the leadership crew for a prominent company that sold appliances on a retail and contract basis. The contract division would voyage to trade shows to display the newest and shiniest kitchen equipment to prospective builders and renovators. We would not allow cameras in the booth, but the Chinese competitors would arrive in great numbers and huddle around a particular product like a fleet of pirate ships closing in on a merchant vessel. They would sketch the dimensions and control panels of our products including, on one occasion, an over-the-range microwave then made in the United States. It should not come as a great shock to know that said microwave disappeared from the United States' manufacturing scene within two years. And ours was not the only booth boarded by the sketching interlopers.

Hunt estimates that businesses between three hundred million dollars and three billion dollars in value are the primary targets of hackers, who no longer need sketch pads to steal powder. Companies over three billion dollars are more than likely to have specialized professionals in place to keep their powder dry. Companies below three hundred million dollars may be boarded easily by bots, but the effort may be deemed less worthwhile by the would-be invaders. The strongest cannons of the enemies will likely be aimed at the companies in the middle because their infiltration, their invisible boarding of the victim's ship, is likely to be possible and profitable, yielding the best booty available. Companies must take extensive precautions to prevent their enemies from boarding. They must keep whatever valuable powder they are holding in reserve dry and safe.

Unleashing the Inner Pyrate in Your World:

How might your company be boarded by bots and what should you do to keep your ship safe? What information do you need to protect?

1.

2.

What do you need to make it happen in your world?

When will you do it?

What is the Prize Worth?

XIII

Know that, as ye approach the vessel. What be ye willing to pay in crew and carnage to yer ship to secure the other vessel? Is that vessel riding high in the water? How full be their hold? Coming from the colonies of Virginia or North Carolina they may carry valuables like tobacco, hogs, cotton, flour, or corn. How many guns can ye see? Even sloops can be dangerous when well-armed and manned by an experienced crew.

Bear in mind that yer target may also have charts and instruments of navigation. Ye can always use good charts and navigational tools.

Bonus Brethren Information

Blackbeard was taught by Ben Hornigold never to underestimate the enemy (1). In the most intense battle of his life, Blackbeard failed to take heed of his mentor's principle and miscalculated the worth of the vessel for which he fought. His target, Lieutenant Maynard's sloop, the Jane, had indeed suffered from the most recent broadside of grapeshot from the Adventure. Twenty men lay wounded and dying on her decks. In a rare blunder, Blackbeard assumed he had won and brought his ship beside the naval sloop, securing the two vessels and leading his crew to board. The pirate captain had miscalculated the numbers of the enemy crew: fourteen surviving members of Maynard's crew lay in wait for the pirates just below deck. Blackbeard and his shipmates quickly found themselves unexpectedly outnumbered on someone else's ship and thus begun a battle, adding unplanned blood to Blackbeard's typically better-balanced ledger.

::: APPLICATION :::

JAB Holding Company

While I hear few reports of the capturing of vessels these days, larger companies do board and take over smaller ones through mergers and acquisitions. Recently, Luxembourg-based JAB Holding Company added Panera Bread to its rapidly-growing armada. The commodore company had acquired Krispy Kreme in 2016 and Einstein Noah Restaurant Group before that. The Panera deal stood out to me not only because I enjoy making port there often (I have lost count of the number of meetings I have held within the friendly atmosphere of Panera locations in my area), but because of the premium (thirty percent) above stock value of the seven point five billion dollar transaction. This was done in part to support the company's most recent investment of forty million dollars in upgrades to systems that increased their outline research. The result was a four percent growth in business, as rare these days in the highly competitive restaurant business as a miscalculation by Blackbeard.

What struck me even more about this deal was the cleverness

of both sides in seeing the potential benefits to each of them. As I coasted on the airwaves of my television set, I caught an interview on CNN's Financial News wherein Ron Shaich, Panera's founder, chairman, and CEO, revealed what could be the secret behind the success of the deal (2). What was JAB Holding Company's treasure that Shaich found valuable enough to trade for his captaincy of an independent Panera?

JAB could ensure smoother sailing. JAB Holding Company had the loyalty of investors whose commitments went back centuries rather than mere decades. Additionally, going private and submitting to a corporate commodore allowed Shaich to do two things he could not as a captain sailing solo. For one, decisions could be made with far greater ease because fewer people would be involved in the decision-making process in private culture, hence speeding up response time. Second, Shaich celebrated a different kind of freedom, the freedom to devote his time to what he does best (3). Thus, Shaich understood that stability was well worth the independence of his ship. JAB Holding Company had the sense to see that the true cost of the acquisition was worth more than dollars and cents. Meanwhile, the commodore company added a valuable vessel to its fleet, one that was already sailing toward greater growth.

The course of mergers and acquisitions does not always run smoothly, however, and some companies fail to heed Blackbeard's warning and example. One such failure that continues to enthrall me was the merger of Time Warner and America Online (AOL). Failing to factor in what lay just beyond the horizons when calculating the worth of their merger, the two companies attempted in 2001 to transform themselves into the place where the waters of the old and the new join together to surge forward into a brighter future. Their ill-conceived consolidation cost one hundred sixty-four billion dollars, a sum they hoped would pale in comparison to the great bounty of their "revolutionary" merger.

In truth, the merger was bound to be shark bait. The cultures of the two companies were as mismatched as cutlass with a cannon fight. The dot-com bubble burst and dial-up internet access began to decline, sending the newly-unified fleet of Time Warner and AOL into an unforeseen and costly storm. Weary and battered, AOL/Time Warner reported a forty-five-billion-dollar write-down in 2003. Their gross miscalculation of value led to a hundred-billion-dollar yearly loss. In 2009, the two companies at last saw the error of their ways and parted, both again sailing solo, rather worse for wear.

Unleashing the Inner Pyrate in Your World:

If your company or organization is looking to expand, how can you apply the lessons of Blackbeard and his present-day echoes to the calculation of the costs and benefits of your expansion?

1.

2.

What do you need to make it happen in your world?

When will you do it?

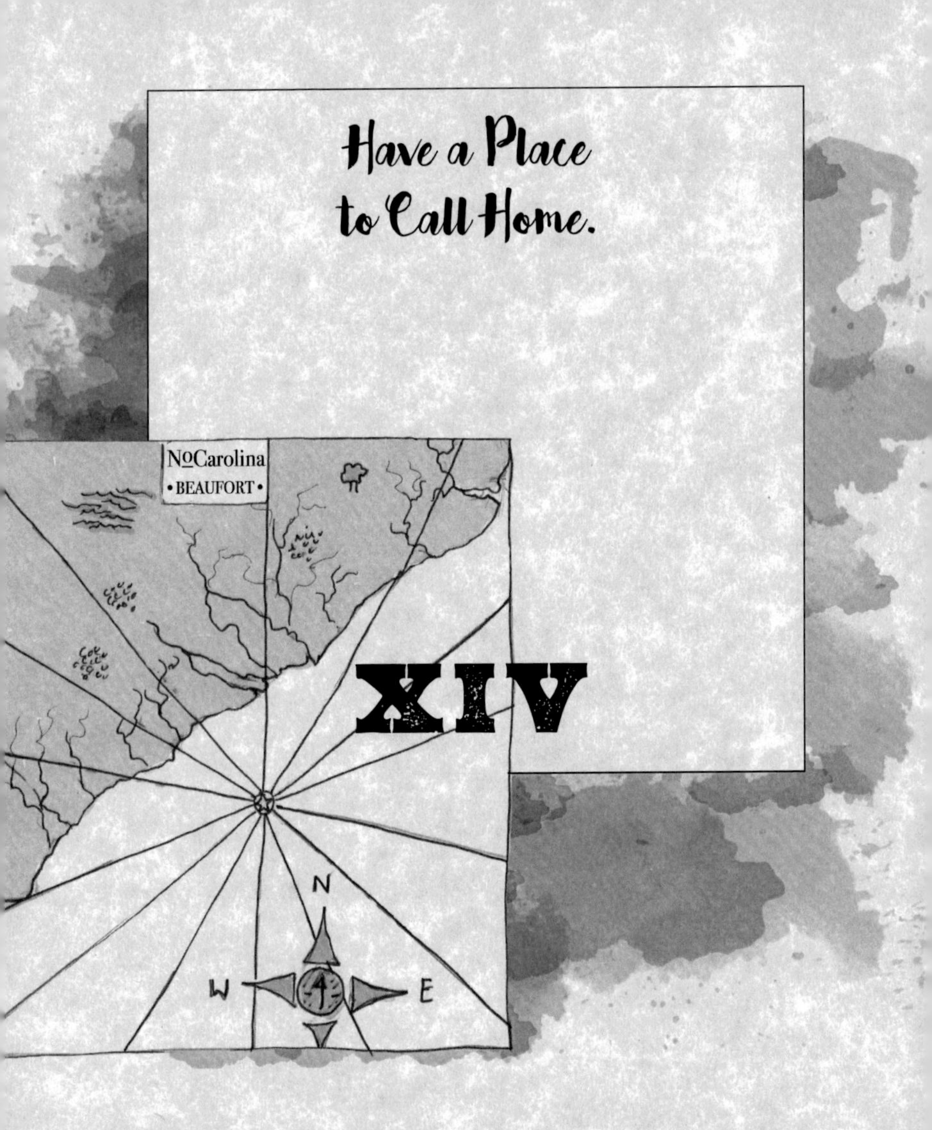

As ye read these words, ye may ask yerselves why I chose to come to Ocracoke. A sheltered bay off the Pamlico Sound, Ocracoke is the perfect place to dock and rest and recover from wounds. Simple as that. No one lived there and 'tis protected by the Atlantic Ocean to the East and the very challenging Pamlico Sound to the West. Uncertain depths make it difficult to navigate and thus provide me with an edge o'er others coming to the island. On the shores of Ocracoke we can rest easy and get ready fer our next adventure.

Bonus Brethren Information

The freedom pirates experienced at sea came at a high price. Their new social order hadn't yet had the time to become stable and establish any structure of significance on land. Crews were more comfortable at sea, it seems, especially once New Providence, their sole gathering place, had fallen into the hands of stricter British authorities and was no longer a safe haven for the now-hounded pirates.

Ocracoke, intended as a new pirate haven wherein crews could make port and find unconditional acceptance and safety, became the site of Blackbeard's downfall rather than a haven for him and his brethren. Left without a place to rest and replenish their supplies and crews or hold Brethren councils safely, the fierce independence of Golden Age pirates did them little good. With nowhere to run but the open sea, pirates became easy targets for authorities in hot pursuit (1).

::: APPLICATION :::

Safe Haven Kids Emergency Shelter

Angela (Pina) Ridling of Texas understands the value of a place to call home. At the age of sixteen, Ridling was asked to leave her home when she refused to marry an older man. Attempting to navigate the world on her own, Ridling was met with an ocean of difficulties and trials. Tougher and older, she returned to South Texas after thirty years away and set her course for keeping other children from being tossed overboard without a place to make port.

Joined by like-minded Dalia Lopez, Ridling sought to establish a safe haven in the Rio Grande Valley for children in the foster care system, children against whom the decks are usually stacked. In 2015, seventeen thousand three hundred seventy-eight children were removed from their Texas homes and placed on the unsteady decks of the foster care system. In Texas, seventy four percent of foster children wind up in prison by the time they reach the age of twenty-five. Professionals who chart plans for prisons take into account the number of children in foster care when considering the best locations for facilities. With no place to dock safely, foster children are easily swept up by the winds of poor influences and marooned by the choices they were forced to make in their unsheltered youth.

In 2015, Ridling began to build a better option for Texan foster children in an area with no shelter within two hundred fifty miles. To do so, though, she needed an available port, a house for the children to call home. She found her haven in the form of a six-bedroom, five-bathroom house that had remained on the market without many worthy offers for longer than the owners wished. And so Ridlings and the homeowners struck an accord and Safe Haven found its Ocracoke Island.

Housing up to twenty-five children from newborns to those aged ten, Safe Haven is a refuge for children who have been removed from their homes and need immediate protection due to abuse, neglect, or abandonment. Volunteers have shown up on Safe Haven's shores since its establishment and continue to provide whatever help is needed. Captained by Ridling, Safe Haven provides a secure, loving environment wherein the children can rest and recuperate from the already arduous journeys of their lives. They can heal from the wounds of their past and learn to trust adults again, adults who help them transform their lives for the better and brighten their horizons.

Unlike the pirates of the past, Ridling is joined in her efforts, rather than being opposed, by governmental authorities. Child Protective Services and Hidalgo County will be working with Ridling in 2018 to increase the number of children the haven can help and open another facility to house children from ages twelve to eighteen, perhaps even aiding such children to stay afloat through college. Harkening back to Blackbeard's principle of apprenticeship, Ridling also aims one day to provide technology training and links to jobs for those who age out of the system, providing them with the tools necessary to build their own stable homes, their own individual safe havens.

Ridling marvels at the strides she and her fleet of volunteers have already made for the next generation and steadfastly sails toward securing such children an even better future, praying that the winds blow in her favor. Whatever the horizon holds for her, Ridling gives all the credit to God for making her vision a reality.

Unleashing the Inner Pyrate in Your World:

What is home to you? How has this story touched your heart and inspired you to share your ideas of home or help others find theirs?

1.

2.

What do you need to make it happen in your world?

When will you do it?

Failure is Not an Option

XV

Ye love the Sea in yer face, the excitement of the chase, the taking of the prize. Ye are Alive – nothing else matters. Ye love the Freedom that comes from the Life ye have chosen. To keep all this protected, there is no room fer failure, fer failure will get ye a trip to Davy Jones's Locker, perhaps after a hempen jig.

Bonus Brethren Information

Although the Crown had extended its hand of peace through a series of pardons, many pirates had chosen not to accept. The risk of remaining true to the Brethren of the Coast, well elucidated by the words of Blackbeard, was very real. British authorities executed between four and six hundred pirates between the years 1716 and 1726. They isolated pirates from their allies as well, starving them out by criminalizing any association with them. Anyone caught conducting business of any sort or even fraternizing with pirates promptly met the same fate as their seafaring friends: execution (1).

North Carolina was home to some exceptional escapees of this sad fate. Blackbeard himself, for instance, had an interesting relationship with Governor Eden and Tobias Knight. Try as they might, the critics of these two men – those who suspected that they were in cahoots with pirates – were never successful in pursuing them through legal means. Blackbeard no doubt was careful in whom he trusted on shore. He had the trust of these two (2).

::: APPLICATION :::

Diane Hendricks, ABC Supply Co. Inc.

In the supercharged world of roofing supply, flagship ABC Supply Co. Inc. leads the charge. What perhaps separates ABC from many of its competitors is the attitude that begins with the captain at the top of the leadership ladder and is passed down through the crew, one level at a time. Roofing is a commodity product and is available in multiple locations around the United States. All the big boxes carry various recognizable brands, as well as regional and some national players. But, the one that stands out among all the players is ABC Supply Co. Inc. It has been my personal experience over the years, with a background in building materials and sales to the building trades in my travels, to have on multiple occasions encountered or done business with ABC locations in the Southeast. For those who are curious to see how different this company is from the rest of the fleet of roofing supply companies, one needs only to visit a location.

Just one voyage to a local branch will provide proof-positive that ABC's philosophy is working and working well. Scattered across the United States, there are seven hundred fifteen convenient locations to choose from. Once there, one will find courteous, knowledgeable crew members whose focus is on the customers and what challenge they may bring on a given day. They share a great can-do attitude. What separates ABC from its armada of competitors is its employees' appreciation for where they work, and the feeling is mutual.

This mutual appreciation was most recently demonstrated as clearly as a Jolly Roger framed by the rising sun. ABC Supply Co. Inc. was recognized for the tenth time and awarded the Gallup Great Workplace Award. This treasure is no mere trinket of a trophy. It is an acknowledgement of the world's top workplaces for employee engagement which Gallup describes as "being emotionally invested in, and focused on, creating value for the organization." Such are the values in which ABC Supply Co.'s captain, Chairman Diane Hendricks, takes great pride (3).

For Co-founder and now Chairman Diane Hendricks, the voyage to success and her understanding of the great value of engendering trust in one's crew began on a dairy farm with eight sisters. She wanted to work outside among the muck and mire of the dairy farm, but her father said no. Then she was swept up in the winds of change.

Hendricks found herself with child at seventeen, a surprise followed by a short marriage that set her off on a journey to Beloit, Wisconsin. As with many young women in that area, she found herself as a crew member for the Parker Pen Company, assembling fountain pens similar to the one I still use today. After her divorce, the now-single mom needed to expand her horizons and began to sell real estate, earning her broker's license. Sailing into a whole new world, Hendricks, the hard-working single mom saw networking opportunities arise. Among those she met on this newly-successful solo voyage was a roofing contractor, Ken Hendricks. She had discovered someone in whom she could risk placing her trust. The two formed an alliance, becoming partners, buying up distressed houses, renovating them, and then renting them.

The tides of Hendricks's life had changed for the better. She and Ken were married in 1975 and then expanded their horizons by adding industrial buildings to their holdings. They saw potential. With more rental units being added, they decided to add more industrial property (4). The couple voyaged to a banker in nearby Janesville, Wisconsin, to finance a purchase and were told, "We don't do business with entrepreneurs, and we don't want your business." They returned to Beloit, and the rest is history. There they built their own ship in the form of ABC Supply Co. Inc. in 1982. The roofing distributor has been growing ever since.

The mission of ABC Supply is focused. But one needn't just take my word for it. The mission statement, the flag they fly on their website, boasts that they aim to be "the biggest, best and easiest service company distributing select interior and exterior building products. We will be recognized as an employee-first company producing world-class associate engagement, customer engagement and financial results." (5)

And their code, the core values that guide them as such articulations once guided the pirates of the past? ABC Supply Co.'s articles are sevenfold. The code that that they believe will make them the best company to work for in America is comprised of these planks:

- Respect
- Opportunity
- "Work Hard, Have Fun"
- Entrepreneurial Spirit
- Family
- Give Back
- American Pride

Once ABC was established, life did not simply become smooth sailing for Mrs. Hendricks. Near Christmas, 2007, I got a call from one of my friends who worked with ABC Supply near my home port. My friend launched a sad tale: Ken Hendricks, while inspecting some work on the roof of his home, had fallen through and later died from his injuries. To add to this personal tragedy of Mrs. Hendricks, her family, and the company, the U.S. economy went into a tailspin, devastating the construction industry and leaving it in worse shape than a vessel ravaged by cannon fire.

With all the personal drama as well as unprecedented pressure on the construction industry, locals in Beloit, Wisconsin, where ABC Supply Co. is headquartered, were concerned that Mrs. Hendricks would sell the company and abandon the pending plans to restore part of the town. That did not happen. Instead, the steadfast captain bought out her biggest competitor, Bradco, and continued her commitment to the community as well. The expansion of ABC Supply Co. caused its fleet to expand from six hundred locations to seven hundred fifteen, and today it continues to thrive. Mrs. Hendricks has shown that on her ship, trust runs upstream as well, proving herself a trustworthy and reliable captain even in the rockiest of waters.

While the couple still held the company's helm together, they found opportunities to not only partner with other entrepreneurs, but also funded the Beloit Film Festival. Even with the loss of her husband, Mrs. Hendricks continues to see opportunities where others see only distress. For her, failure is not an option.

It is impossible to know what really drives people, what gets them up and motivates them in the morning even when the sea churns threateningly beneath their feet. The world outside of her captain's cabin receives few words from Mrs. Hendricks. What the world witnesses are her actions. Under her steady captaincy, ABC Supply Co. Inc. has flourished, even in stormy seas. Her vision is transforming a community, Beloit, one building at a time. In doing so, captain Hendricks is creating safe places for startups to dock and creating jobs for a once-beleaguered city. In the case of Mrs. Hendricks, actions speak louder than words.

Whether building a company or rebuilding a community, ABC Supply's captain remains focused on people. Few persons have the vision that Mrs. Hendricks has to achieve both and somehow thrive in the process. Blackbeard would have been proud to have known her. Faced with incredible odds, she has never considered failure as an option.

Unleashing the Inner Pyrate in Your World:

How has this inspirational story of one focused woman encouraged you to fight on in the face of failure?

1.

2.

What do you need to make it happen in your world?

When will you do it?

Fight Smartly, Lads - and When in a Fight, Steady On and Don't Lose Yer Head

XVI

Stay clear-headed. Be wise in the amount of drink. When the hair in yer nostrils singes from the smoke o' battle and those about ye be caught up in the conflict and confusion, stay focused on the job at hand. I carry six pistols because ye can ne'er have enough pistols handy, and with cutlasses slashing about, 'tis easy to get distracted. Remember to fight back-to-back, allowing no quarter. If ye surrender, yer end will come quickly at the end of a rope.

When facing a man-o'-war, use yer speed and maneuverability. Stay at angles. Avoid broadsides. Heavy guns come into range at over three miles.

In the case of an armed merchant, show yer colours. If there be no response, then fire a shot across their forefoot. If there still be no response, approach the stern first. If she has aft-facing guns, approach with yer bow first. A more narrow target. If no guns aft, then come about and use yer fore guns to hit her rudder and take away her ability to maneuver. Yer swivel guns with swan and partridge shot will clear that area of the deck.

Once ye have boarded yer prey and are approached in a fight, be wise and fight, best you can, with your backside to the backside of a shipmate. Ye can circle as needed, using first yer pistols, then cutlasses, keeping the enemy at bay or inflicting great harm. Yer backside is covered.

Yer shipmate covers ye and ye cover him. What be ye there to do? Take the other ship. Then do it, take the other ship.

Bonus Brethren Information

Perhaps when Blackbeard penned this, he had no inkling about the climactic battle to come off Ocracoke Island. The two vessels sent by Lieutenant Governor Spotswood arrived off North Carolina's Outer Banks on November 21, 1718. With one boat disabled, Lieutenant Robert Maynard commanded the Ranger as it entered the inlet that evening and sighted Blackbeard's Adventure anchored in open water. The ensuing battle was joined by more British forces at daybreak, after the Royal Navy jettisoned much of its ballast.

Maynard had the Union Jack run up on his previously unidentified vessel. In response, Blackbeard raised his personal black ensign with a horned skeleton. After receiving cannon fire, Maynard's crew, not equipped with cannon, answered with musket volleys and then hid below decks in a ruse to lure the pirates aboard the English vessel. Maynard later wrote of his adversary that "at our first Salutation, he drank Damnation to me and my Men, whom he stil'd Cowardly Puppies, saying, He would neither give or take Quarter."" (1)

Deceived by the seamen's stratagem, Blackbeard, not taking his own advice, led his crew and clambered aboard the Ranger. They were immediately surrounded and ultimately vanquished by Maynard's men, who emerged from the hold. In the ensuing chaos in which the sea around the vessel was described by a contemporary as "tinctur'd with Blood," Maynard and Blackbeard came face to face.

Blackbeard should have heeded his own advice. When he led his depleted and hung-over crew aboard the Jane, he went after Captain Maynard without any backup. As Maynard emerged from the ship's hold, he faced the storming pirate. Maynard's sword was drawn and thrust toward Blackbeard. Blackbeard's cutlass then shattered Maynard's sword up the hilt, cutting his hand. Maynard responded by firing his pistol point blank. Blackbeard, still standing, prepared to deliver a death blow to his enemy. His back remained unguarded. The helmsman, a Scottish Highlander, immune to the carnage, approached Blackbeard from the rear and slashed the fearsome captain's face, nearly taking off his head before being repelled. With Blackbeard's crew now falling all about and no one to cover his back, he lurched forward in a hail of pistol shot from the Navy seaman.

The legend was dead. He did not fight smartly. Later it was discovered that he had sustained twenty-five wounds, five of which were from pistol balls. "Here was an end to that courageous brute, who might have passed in the world for a hero had he been employed in a good cause," remarked a contemporary.

Almost immediately, Maynard had the pirate's head severed and hung the grisly trophy from the bowsprit of the Ranger. The rest of Blackbeard's corpse was thrown overboard after which, according to legend, it swam defiantly several times around the sloop. Stopping first at Bath Towne, North Carolina, Maynard discovered much of the pirates' booty in the barn of Tobias Knight, Governor Eden's secretary. With the recovered goods on board and Blackbeard's skull swinging from the bowsprit, the expedition returned to Virginia (2).

::: APPLICATION :::

In Blackbeard's day, a hostile takeover at sea was less than subtle. While shots across the bow are frowned upon on Wall Street today, that doesn't mean the takeovers are not dramatic. There is abundant evidence that all is not quiet on 'The Street.' A recent article from the Harvard Review reveals a rise in hostile and unsolicited mergers and acquisitions. For instance, hostile takeover bids rose from five percent of merger and acquisition volume in 2013 to eleven percent in 2015, the latter representing five hundred sixty three billion dollars, that is billion with a B like "buccaneer."

Among the fleet of familiar names bandied about in the business headlines recently were twenty-first Century Fox's offer for Time Warner, which was withdrawn; Cigna's bid for Anthem, which sent shock waves through the healthcare community; and DISH Network's bid for Spirit Nextel, which, like twenty-first Century Fox, was withdrawn.

In the waters of the Caribbean when Blackbeard approached with his distinctive flag fluttering in the gathering breeze, the rules were simple to follow:

1. Flee from the faster vessel.
2. If fleeing is not possible, stand and fight.
3. In the face of defeat, drop sails and surrender.

The same simple principles could be applied to the Boards of Directors for today's top conglomerates when facing attack.

For starters, the captains of a company can just reject the offer outright. Period. This often happens when the offer is above the current stock price. The response from the potential buyer could also be simple: the point is to seek out those stockholders who are major players and woo them specifically, or appeal directly to the stockholders in general, hoping to garner the backing of the majority. Certainly, contacting and soliciting the stockholders is a big challenge, but with billions in the balance, justification could take over. If the current Board has been a good fit for stockholders and is held in high esteem, this strategy by the prospective buyer attempting to board will probably fail. If the Board has done a poor job in directing the company, this tactic could be successful.

Just what is a hostile takeover? It is one company's attempt to acquire another company by acquiring a representative percentage of the company and voting shares, or by directing efforts to stockholders, or to gain control. This is called a proxy fight. Regardless of the tactics used, the Board of Directors is put on notice and comes to the table with ideas, perhaps long overdue ideas for a change.

Boards can respond with any of a variety of strategies. They may return fire with the use of what is called differential voting rights (DVR). That means that stockholders with fewer voting rights are paid an increased dividend, adding an incentive for those folks or institutions not to support the takeover. Following the style of Blackbeard and his colleagues in treating all crew alike, the Board could create an employee stock ownership program (ESOP), with the net result that employees, the crew, would own a substantial interest in the company and thus be motivated to follow the leadership of the captains of the company.

"A more drastic method is known as a shareholder rights plan, or a 'poison pill' defense, which allows existing shareholders to buy newly issued stock at a discount if one shareholder has bought more than a stipulated percentage of the stock – and the buyer who triggered the defense is excluded from the discount. The term is often used broadly to include a range of defenses, including issuing both additional debt to make the target less attractive and stock options to employees that vest upon a merger.

A 'people pill' (a variation on the 'poison pill') provides for the resignation of key personnel in the case of a hostile takeover, while the 'Pac-Man defense' has the target company aggressively buy stock in the company attempting the takeover" (3). Pirate captains were familiar with this sort of strategy, for it parallels one way they could be voted out as captain.

One mode of operation that may help prevent a hostile takeover is for senior leadership to keep the Board of Directors focused and creative, providing their company with clear direction for the future. It is preferred by contemporary captains to have those creative juices flowing in the boardroom, rather than their blood on the deck. They may discover other companies in the market that are aligned with them and would be potential partners. They can battle back to back, applying their strengths to the others' weaknesses and visa versa. Or the new allies could stop competing in common markets with shrinking market share and pool their resources against other competitors. In the process they may find commonality from a leadership perspective.

Unleashing the Inner Pyrate in Your World:

What two ideas have come to you as part of the leadership team in dealing with threats to your company as you read through this Principle?

1.

2.

What do you need to make it happen in your world?

When will you do it?

Don't Be Afraid to Board the Hunted

XVII

The Treasure is there awaiting ye. Ye must go and get it. Let yer flagg tell who is coming, and yer cannon signal that ye be serious beyond their wildest imagination. Let yer muskets clear the deck of those who are foolish enough to stand in yer way.

Ye or yer Quartermaster be the first over the gunnel – it matters not soe much what ye say, because they canna hear ye in combat, but yer crew can see ye over the rail and on the deck of the other ship leading the way, a sgian dubh in yer teeth, pistols in both hands, with cutlasses to follow.

Bonus Brethren Information

Risk was always present for pirate ships. The notorious Charles Vane was an example of not leading, regardless of risk. Cruel beyond description in how he often treated those he captured, in November, 1718, he found his ship approaching another ship. He ran up his colors only to discover the other vessel was a French man-of-war, that responded with a broadside. To the dismay of most of his crew, he withdrew, not willing to take the risk of attacking and boarding the other ship. The next day the majority of his crew voted to have him removed from being captain, accusing him of cowardice and replacing him with Jack Rackham, who had been his quartermaster. Vane and a few crew who were on his side were set afloat in a small sloop. Life would never be the same for Vane, and he was soon captured by the authorities and executed (1). Risk has its rewards.

::: APPLICATION :::

Vanderhall Motor Works, Inc.

Risks today are not nearly as breathtaking as those taken in Blackbeard's day by the captain and his contemporaries. Today, risk takers are often visionaries who can see what others cannot even imagine. Two vocations spring quickly to my mind when I think of the brave buccaneers of this century. Farmers, by nature, look at fields as opportunities to do what they love to do and see crops coming to harvest on their horizons. Many steps, untold hours, and much risk – from storms to freezes to infestations – bring food to tables across the globe. The other vocation that involves risk as regularly as that faced by pirates is the business of building homes. They too need to be visionaries, looking at a piece of earth and imagining a home being built, again with risk of weather, the economy, a growing array of regulations, and regional trends, plus fluctuating costs that border sometimes on madness. And yet they continue to build. The world needs both vocations.

Close in their boat wake, there is the industry that replaced ships and other sea vessels: ground transportation, getting from here to there across the United States. Is the risk too great for innovation in this highly competitive realm? Some members of the driving public may be getting a little bored with the same basic body styles used by many manufacturers. What if something really different sailed out into the marketplace for those who wanted to fall in love with simply driving again? That would be risky for the manufacturer, but potentially as exhilarating for drivers as feeling the spray of the ocean on their faces and the wind in their sails.

As part of the research for this chapter, I asked a simple question of Daniel Boyer, director of sales and marketing for risk-taking company Vanderhall Motor Works Inc.: "What does your business do?" He replied, smooth as the surface of a calm sea, "Vanderhall designs, builds, and manufactures motoring passion."

For the most fortunate, the introduction to Vanderhall begins with a test drive at a local dealership (they have seventeen dealerships in ten states), which will have an armada of cars on display. Local drivers are invited to come slip behind the wheel and take a Vanderhall product for a spin.

And so it was for me. An innocent late Sunday afternoon journey to a local dining spot took a potentially risky turn when my wife suggested we stop at a dealership of a brand with which I was yet unfamiliar. Thinking that the name "Vanderhall" trips nicely off the tongue, I had no concept of what they offer to the driving public. We soon found out.

After filling out the required releases, my wife and I found ourselves inside a dark red Venice model, number three in the tour of four vehicles that was about to start. The model we drove was automatic, with the dealer-installed bump shift option. Tightly turned to the right, we headed out, testing brakes as we went. Bikers will love the brakes on a Vanderhall: they stop with attitude. The wide-tracked tires keep the vehicle poised. We made a quick right-hand turn from the parking lot and followed our flagship, who got enough ahead for us to see if the 1.4 liter supercharged engine was as advertised. It was quick. We meandered through back streets and neighborhoods, staying within the posted speed limit of twenty-five, then to connecting streets where we went to forty-five miles per hour.

It was a lovely early autumn afternoon, fit for sailing on the high seas or taking a spin on land. A nice breeze was working its way around the windscreen of the open-topped roadster. Beneath the surface of my calm demeanor on this pleasant day lay a hidden agenda: to take my borrowed land-vessel to a serious stretch of road and see what she could do. The flagship of our pack of four read my mind, and soon we were headed toward the Interstate. We merged onto I-40 during a busy part of the afternoon and were cut off by another car, breaking our little convoy. Not an issue. At forty-five miles-per-hour I stayed close by. While watching traffic from the left-hand lane, I saw an opportunity on my horizon and veered left into an open lane. In doing so, I hit the accelerator with a vengeance and we went from forty-five to eighty in two and a half car lengths. I felt the rush of the nice boost of power and incredible control. I merged safely behind the speeding other two members of our party. As we all prepared to exit, I was hooked. This was a fun car, a roadster or autocycle to be more accurate. I wanted to know more about this all-American car from Provo, Utah.

Delving deeper into this newfound flagship in the automotive industry, I found that cars are becoming more and more utilitarian. Vanderhall seeks to stem the tide of motorized automation with a pure connected driving experience. The driver is one with the vehicle; it becomes an extension of them.

There are risks here, just as in Blackbeard's day – risks to reputation, capital, and sanity. Risk is particularly huge from a financial standpoint. The sheer amount of capital required to research, prototype, and later build a factory is enormous. There is no assurance of profit or gain. The added risk of developing a new idea and giving it shape, in this case a vehicle in a marketplace flooded with vehicles, and seeing the concept accepted, is great.

The driving force behind this risky venture is captain Steve Hall, who comes by this behavior and the drive to innovate through his DNA. His grandfather, H. Tracey Hall, invented the process to grow synthetic diamonds that are used in the oil industry. H. Tracey's son, Steve's father, David Hall, is the largest patent holder in Utah. So Steve Hall, with a mind focused on motoring, began a different look at transportation early on, bent on creating something new. His background as a successful, independent, high-end vehicle dealer helped him set sail on his new adventure, and Hall decided to combine his passion for creation with his love of motorsports, and there arose Vanderhall Motor Works, Inc.

What was missing from the process was Hall's penchant for tinkering, and so he began to do so on the side. Eventually, he determined that this creation process would either lead him to a successful product that he could produce and distribute, or he would learn from the attempt. He sold his dealership and set a new course. Hall spent the next six years creating prototypes until he felt like he had found the right formula of timeless design and effortless performance. Risk for this craftsman in carbon to display his creation to the public is no different from the painter who, drawing upon his soul, puts life on canvas for the world to see (and whose work might someday be deemed worthy of risks and might even be stolen by pirates).

Vanderhall's website contains a fascinating history of how Hall shaped the design now in production. Motoring aficionados will enjoy a blend of the history of three-wheeled vehicles, coupled with real-world application of new technology, with a flair for respected tradition. Each Laguna, custom-made for its owner, is hand-crafted by a crew of sixteen skilled artisans, giving shape to carbon fiber as the platform. It takes about three to four months for this to come together. The Venice, my favorite of Vanderhall's vessels, has fewer options and requires only about a week. Regardless, it just may be worth the wait for those who want to set off in a shiny new vessel and explore the world of motoring in a different way.

Vanderhall's goal is to bring consumers back to the golden age of motoring – without the hassles of that age – when driving was an outing rather than the means to reach one's intended port. The company is now charting a course for its future, including a recent groundbreaking plan for a one million square foot factory.

This new expansion will enable growth upwards of twenty-five thousand units per year, and create nine hundred jobs for those seeking to join Vanderhall's crew. Blackbeard would admire Steve Hall's creative approach to finding undiscovered treasure in the marketplace, risk and all.

Unleashing the Inner Pyrate in Your World:

Risk is what faces many leaders, regardless of where they are in a company. What ideas have been spurred by this Principle that you can use?

1.

2.

What do you need to make it happen in your world?

When will you do it?

Final Comments from Your Humble Captain

Twenty-five years of reading and research have gone into this book you are holding. Much has been learned about Blackbeard and his "Brethren of the Coast." Much still remains to be learned. One of the hidden benefits has been the great number of people and personalities that have come my way in the process. I am grateful for each one. My life is richer for having learned from Captain Blackbeard, and I trust you have been enriched by him as well. Now I bid you safe travels as you set off to implement what I have learned and shared, and to help transform some companies and lives.

Over the horizon

There are Principles waiting in the wings to be shared with you.

Staying Moored in Your Home Port:

Further Guidance for the Seafarer Seeking to Understand the Importance of Products Being Made on American Shores

According to Consumer Reports, almost eight in ten American consumers would rather buy an American-made product than an imported one, and over sixty percent say they'd be willing to pay up to ten percent more for it. Why? There are several probable reasons, including trust in American quality or safety, and a desire to support the American economy and American workers. And yet U.S.-produced products seem to be in decline and jobs are going overseas. But is that really the case?

Some very visible products, such as the growing array of electronics, are not made domestically. And look at the labels in your closet. Where were your clothes made? Reversing the trend, however, some appliances and automobiles are again being assembled or even made from scratch in the U.S. Since 2010, about three hundred fifty companies have returned to the U.S., according to the Reshoring Initiative, an industry-supported not-for-profit that focuses on bringing manufacturing jobs back.

Some analysts say that the "Made in America" frontier lies in "brainfacturing" – innovative research in the realms of digital technology, automation, and new materials. In certain industries, such as software, American companies are so dominant that other countries are enacting legislation to lessen their reliance on our technology (1).

The Federal Trade Commission has issued standards for products to bear a "Made in the U.S.A." label, but those guidelines aren't widely understood, nor do consumers know what to do about products that say "assembled" or "designed" in America, or "imported by" a company with an American name and address. The skeptic in me suspects that there is outright deception by companies that slap Americana on their products in hopes they'll be able to cash in on public sentiment, since so many of us won't read the fine print. Be wise as you shop if you are committed to supporting those who manufacture what is truly made in the United States.

Websites for the Voyager on the Waves of the Internet: A Map for Those Who Wish to Sail Further and Seek More Information.

II

www.nsaspeaker.org/contact/

www.ocwwinfo7333.wildapricot.org/

III

www.BlytheLeonard.com

www.highpoint.edu

XII

Steve Hunt, Distinguished Fellow ISSA

IX

www.kentuckyale.com

XI

www.marketgraphicsresearch.com

www.themarketedge.com

XIV

www.safehavenforkids.org

www.abcsupply.com

www.VanderhallUSA.com

Trumpeting for Counsel:

A Collection of Quotes from and about These Captains and Commodores

A Brief Note on Blackbeard:

- "I haven't see one single piece of evidence that Blackbeard ever used violence against anyone" - Trent University historian Arne Bialuschweski
- "Damnation seize my soul if I give you quarter, or take any from you" - Blackbeard, as recorded by Captain Charles Johnson
- "[I]n the commonwealth of pirates, he who goes the greatest length for wickedness is looked upon with a kind of envy amongst them, as a person of more extraordinary gallantry, and is thereby entitled to be distinguished by some post, if such a one has but courage, he must certainly be a great man. The hero of whom we are writing [Blackbeard] was thoroughly accomplished this way, and some of his frolics of wickedness, were so extravagant, as if he aimed at making his men believe he was a devil incarnate…" - Captain Charles Johnson, *A General History of the Pyrates*

Unpacking the Treasure Chest…:

- "Puritan ministers and legitimate sea captains, with the aid of contemporary writers, are largely responsible for the popular conception of pirates. If a captain lost his ship to a pirate crew, he would be depended upon to exaggerate the depravity and wickedness of the pirates, and any embellishments would enhance his own reputation and make it easier for him to gain control of another ship" - Wake Forest University law professor Robert Lee

I

- "Milk gets us in the door" - Rob Armstrong
- "It's been over thirty years since my father decided to retire. At the time, we were seriously considering closing our doors. But when we looked at the Munroe team, we saw a tremendously dedicated core of people who believed in our company and understood our value to the community. We held off closing, and our crew hung in there. For the next three years, we strapped up and arrived at the dairy at two a.m. while doubling our delivery routes. The sacrifices – undeniably selfless – made all the difference. Looking back, it's amazing what a great core of employees will do. They are the reason we have been able to stay in business after

[one hundred and thirty five] years" - Rob Armstrong, interviewed with Providence Business Daily News

- "If you want to make something happen, start with the people you hire. To be a milkman, you have to have a servant heart. You need to care about the people you serve daily. If you are lucky enough to find these individuals, make sure to take care of them, because they are the ones who demonstrate the company's values to your customers… We have always sought to bring value into the lives of every customer we service. Be sure to give the time, effort, and energy to the individuals who keep your business running. Effort produces value, and value creates loyalty" - Rob Armstrong, ibid.

III

- "One of the best parts for me, just personally, is being able to walk into a factory in Middlesex, N.C. and talk to men and women that have jobs now, that are working. To be able to talk to women that have been sewing for thirty years, and walk me through changes to a sweatshirt that are going to make it better because of the knowledge that she has" - Bayard Winthrop
- "Buying American made is the new haute couture. Buy local… support each other and keep the economy supported in your own area" - Blythe Leonard
- "Folks want to know more about where their products come from" - Kelly Nester, President of Nester Hosiery of Mt. Airy, NC
- "Consumers are hungry for a sense of community. Local goods have a distinctive character and an appealing sense of authenticity," - University of Michigan's Ross School of Business professor Rajeev Batra, Ph.D.

IV

- "...that said Negroes being taken on Board a Pyrate vessell and by what appears equally concerned with the rest of the Crew in the Same Acts of Piracy ought to be Try'd in the same Manner, and if any diversity appears in their Circumstances the same may be considered on their Tryal" -the ruling Council during the trial of Blackbeard's crew
- "I want us to get to a place where the workers here can make enough to live a lifestyle that is dignified and worthy as humans" - Niki Okuk, interviewed by Kai Ryssdal on American Public Media's "Marketplace"
- "There about 22 gallons of oil in each truck tire, so that number means we've cleaned up a volume of petroleum greater than the Exxon-Valdez spill" - Niki Okuk, ibid.

- "I grew up in L.A. Right out of college I had an idea that I wanted to work in development, go all over the world and help developing countries with economic policy or stimulus, but you kind of get to those places and realize there's a lot of work to be done back at home" - Niki Okuk, ibid.
- **JH:** What are your plans on expanding?
NO: The sky is the limit. I believe Rco^2 can grow by making more rubber products, but we can also grow in different directions, by diversifying into plastics recycling or maybe a whole new field such as soil remediation. It's really up to the crew. As long as we maintain our soul, the company's objective to contribute to the community, uplift its workers, and have a positive impact on the environment - I leave it to the people who work here and will eventually own the company to define how RCO^2 will live into the future, how they will change and create their work and roles, and what they would like to leave their children.
- **JH:** What was the biggest obstacle you have had to overcome to make Rco^2 happen, or keep it going?
NO: I think capital is always the greatest challenge for a start-up. Tire recycling isn't a glamorous Silicon Valley industry and investors weren't looking for us. Despite the myth that the SBA is here for small business the real truth is that public agencies don't invest public tax dollars in speculation, and start-ups are just that. I learned the hard way that you have to have at least 5 years in business to get a real loan. There is another myth that there are funds or resources earmarked for women, minority, & green businesses – even I believed that – but it is simply NOT true. To get Rco^2 started we used personal credit cards, I took several short term high interest loans in the first years, didn't pay myself a salary & was often late on bills and rent. Our first real loan came from the Los Angeles Jewish Free Loan Association who makes zero interest loans to uplift the community as part of their religious practice, it's their mitzvah or tidings. I thought that was incredible: we aren't Jewish or related to the Jewish community in anyway – but they were the only folks who would believe in us and take a leap, I'm eternally grateful to their organization. Most businesses fail because they are under-capitalized, and capital markets have been especially tight since the recession. The best thing any group or agency could do to build more small businesses would be to make capital available to us.
- **JH:** For you, what brings the greatest satisfaction to date?
NO: When I stated Rco^2 I measured our success by environmental metrics, we've recycled more than 300 million pounds of rubber, thereby diverting more than 70 million gallons of oil from landfills. But really, the greatest satisfaction comes from the people who work here. I've watched our people overcome some incredible challenges, some of our people

started out houseless, living in their cars and have now transitioned to stable housing. Some have been picked up on old warrants or lost their children because of bad living situations, and we've helped them get back on their feet and reunite with their families. Our driver recently lost his mother and wife, becoming an orphan and single father at the same time but is now in the process of buying his own home. Our first employee to do so.

- **JH:** What appealed/called to you to start Rco^2? **NO:** I worked in finance out of college but I think I always wanted to start my own business. After my MBA I decided I wanted to do a green business, and I knew I wanted it to be a real brick and mortar business, one that made things, made jobs, and made a real impact - I didn't want a tech or service company. It was with that criteria, to create "green collar jobs" as Van Jones calls them, that I started out looking at plastics recycling, paper recycling, oil or battery recycling.
- **JH:** What is the 2 (as in second power?) significant of as part of your logo? **NO:** It's actually really silly, since our name is just the initials of the founders I added the 2 to make it look like the scientific symbol for carbon dioxide with an R – maybe implying reduced or recycled carbon dioxide. The 2 is in the wrong place so it's not really scientific but the name stuck. We picked a very general name because I want to be able to change and expand, we didn't want to be defined by tires, but rather to be defined by our mission and to remain open to new and different versions of company that might do totally different things in the future, hopefully our name give us that room to grow.
- **JH:** What roles do your employees play in Rco^2? **NO:** Accounting, shipping, receiving, manufacturing (of course), sales, customer service, and IT... Most of our staff are on the warehouse floor where there are several specialized roles. Our equipment is custom and learning how to operate and maintain it is a long learning process however we try to make sure that everyone learns others' roles so that our crew is flexible. For example the punch press operator should train the person who feeds the material into the punch how to grease the machine and change the blades and dies so that they can step up into the operator position if needed. There is a foreman but also 2-3 other people who have been with the company and can step up into the foreman position to direct the flow of work in the yard because they understand where products are loaded and unloaded, and what tasks need to be accomplished every day. At the moment we don't have any administrative staff. I answer phones, invoice customers, print packing slips, however I hope to start training the rest of the crew in my role as well so they can have a broader understanding of the company functions – I would ultimately like them to own the company and they will need to understand front office operations in order to hire someone

competent to conduct them.

- Niki Okuk's interview by SME crew member Jessica Harmon

VI

- "[P]irate communities... democracies. A hundred years before the French Revolution, the companies were run on lines in which liberty, equality, and brotherhood were the rule rather than the exception... At the start of a voyage, or the election of a new captain, a set of written articles was drawn up which every member of the ship's company was expected to sign" - British naval historian David Cordingly

VII

- "I figured I'd do this for six months just to get something local on my résumé so I could look for something else... But I haven't' looked for a job since I stepped foot in here. I don't plan on it" - Zappo's Customer Loyalty Team member Sani Dolan, interviewed in The New York Times Magazine

VIII

- "Winning football games has been more important to me than making money. Winning is what turns me on. Money is pretty good, but a shroud has no pockets" - Robert K. Kraft
- "To start you need to understand we were without a coach for almost a month, and the other coaches had been hired around the league, and they had hired coaching staffs, and I was getting killed for it. Killed. It was toxic. Nobody thought it was a good idea. I was getting killed by the media in Boston. Bill had one winning year in five seasons in Cleveland" - Robert K. Kraft
- "(T)his year, to me, is life. When you want something so badly, you work for it and go through the hard times. You persevere. Our organization hasn't made excuses. But it is what it is. In a way, our fan base has bonded even more with us through the hard times" - Robert K. Kraft
- "Think big. Make it a wildly improbable dream that motivates you, one that wakes you up in the morning ready to attack your day, to persevere and persist until you accomplish it... Dream a big dream, a bold dream. Don't play conservatively between the 40 yard lines. Don't just play it safe" - Robert K. Kraft in his 2016 commencement speech to Yeshiva University graduates

XI

- "Welcome, my name is Dale Akins, President of The Market Edge. Our website is intended to be a resource for every person that earns a living in the construction industry" - The Market Edge website landing page

XIII

- "(A)t the height of the Internet craze, two media companies merged together to form (what was seen as) a revolutionary move to fuse the old with the new. In 2001, old-school media giant Time Warner consolidated with American Online (AOL), the Internet and email provider of the people, for a whopping $164 billion. It was considered a combination of the best of both worlds – but boy was that false!
- Though on paper the merger occurred, the cultures of these two dynamically different companies never did. (unlike that of Panera and JAB Holding Co.) The dot-com bubble burst and the decline of dial-up Internet access spelled disaster for the future. In 2003, AOL/Time Warner reported a $45 billion dollar write-down which led to a $100 billion dollar yearly loss. Finally, in 2009, the two companies finally split in a sort of corporate divorce" - Megan Ruesink in her article "Top Corporate Mergers: The Good, The Bad & The Ugly", (9/28/20115) Megan Ruesink (AUTHOR'S NOTE: This article was originally published in Sept. 2009. It has since been updated to reflect information relevant to 2015)

XIV

- "Try as they might, they were unable to create reliable mechanisms through which they could either replenish their ranks or mobilize their collective strength. These deficiencies of social organization made them, in the long run, relatively easy prey" - Marcus Rediker in his history book Between the Devil and the Deep Blue Sea: Merchant Seamen, Pirates, and Anglo-American Maritime World, 1700-1750
- "It is amazing what we can do when we come together as a community, especially for our children in need. They are our future" - Angela Ridling

Interviews with Jessica Harman.

Endnotes

Foreword

1. Marine Research Society, *The Pirates Own Book*, p. 346.

2. Ibid., p. 348.

Introduction

1. Woodward, Colin, *The Republic of Pirates*, p. 207.

2. Johnson, Captain Charles, *A General History of the Pyrates*, second edition, p. 30.

3. Brooks, Baylus. *Blackbeard Reconsidered*, p. 43.

4. Vallar, Cindy. Blog.

5. Lee, Robert E., *Blackbeard The Pirate*, p. 7.

6. Butler, Lindley S., *Pirates, Privateers, and Rebel Raiders of the Carolina Coast*, p. 13

7. Rediker, Marcus, *Villains of All Nations: Atlantic Pirates in the Golden Age*, p. 151.

8. Ibid., p. 153.

9. Cordingly, David, *Under The Black Flag*, p. 108.

10. Ibid., p. 108.

11. Butler, p. 11.

12. Marx, Jenifer G., "Brethren of the Coast", Chapter 2, p. 36. *A Worldwide Illustrated History of Pirates.*

13. Vallar, Cindy. Blog.

Format of the Book

Pyrate Principle I - Know Yer Home Waters and Use That Knowledge to Yer Advantage

1. *Providence Business News*, December 3, 2015.

2. Ibid., December 3, 2015.

3. Ibid., December 3, 2015.

Pyrate Principle II - Don't Keep All That You Capture – Let Them Go Who Would Enhance Yer Image

1. Marine Research Society, *The Pirates Own Book*, p. 320.
2. Ibid, p. 333.

Pyrate Principle III - Be Distinctive in Yer Personal Style and Presentation

1. Marine Research Society, *The Pirates Own Book*, p. 95
2. National Public Radio Interview, Studio 1A, August 7, 2017.
3. Ibid., August 7, 2017.

Pyrate Principle IV - On the Decks of Me Fleet, All Men Be Equal

1. Kinkor, Kenneth J. "Bandits at Sea a Pirate Reader." *New York University Press.*
2. Ibid., p. 199.
3. Ibid., p. 200.
4. Ibid., p. 200.
5. Ibid., p. 201.
6. Ibid., p. 201.
7. Ibid., p. 201.
8. Ibid., p. 201.
9. Ibid., p. 203
10. Ibid., p. 203
11. Ryssdal, Kai. "Marketplace" NPR/American Public Radio. "*Creating Jobs in Compton by Keeping Old Tires Out of the Landfill.*" Garrova, Robert, writer. , 09 Dec. 2016.

Pyrate Principle V - Apprenticing for the Next Cruize

Interview and correspondence with Roger Clodfelter, Senior Vice President for Communications, High Point University

Pyrate Principle VI - Say What Ye Are Gonna Do, Then Do It

1. Cordingly, David, *Under the Black Flag*, p. 96.
2. New England Pirate Museum, 274 Derby St., Salem, MA, 01970.

Pyrate Principle VII - All Good Plans Include Yer Ship Mates

1. Exquemelin, Alexander, *Buccaneers of America*, 1678.
2. http://www.zappos.com

Pyrate Principle VIII - Be the Captain

1. Marine Research Society, *The Pirates Own Book*, p. 250.
2. Woodward, Colin, *The Republic of Pirates*, p. 319.

Pyrate Principle IX - Be Not Predictable in All Yer Matters

1. Marine Research Society, *The Pirates Own Book*, p. 74.
2. Ibid., p. 412.
3. McMahan, Dana. " Kentucky Monthly". February 2017.

Pyrate Principle X - Fear Not – Show Yer True Colours

1. Marine Research Society, *The Pirates Own Book*, p. 248.
2. Cordingly, David, *Under The Black Flag*, p. 115.
3. Ibid., p. 91-92.
4. Woodward, Colin, *The Republic of Pirates*, p. 287.
5. Cordingly, p. 218.
6. Marilyn Lewendal Interview

Pyrate Principle XI - Eyes to the Horizon – Is It the Enemy or Opportunity?

1. http://www.marketgraphicsresearch.com
2. http://www.themarketedge.com

Pyrate Principle XII - Keep Yer Powder Dry

1. Steve Hunt Interview with Steve Monroe

Pyrate Principle XIII - What Is the Prize Worth?

1. Woodward, Colin, *The Republic of Pirates*, p. 294.
2. CNN Financial News Interview
3. "Fabor Report", April 5, 2017.

Pyrate Principle XIV - Have a Place Called Home

1. Rediker, Marcus, *Villains of All Nations: Atlantic Pirates in the Golden Age*, p. 154.

Pyrate Principle XV - Failure Is Not an Option

1. Rediker, Marcus, *Villains of All Nations: Atlantic Pirates in the Golden Age*, p. 154.
2. Duffus, Kevin, *The Last Days of Blackbeard The Pirate.*
3. ABC Supply press release, May 12, 2016.
4. Kolak, Ben, Jean Yves Chainon, Guglielmo Mattioli, "New York Times", August 7, 2017.
5. http://www.abcsupply.com.

Pyrate Principle XVI - Fight Smartly Lads – And When in a Fight, Steady on and Don't Lose Yer Head

1. Konstam, Angus, Blackbeard, p. 251.
2. Colonial Williamsburg Journal, Vol. 15, No. 1 (Autumn 1992), pp. 22-28.
3. http://www.investopedia.com/terms/h/hostiletakeover.asp#ixzz4dZfzGN8Z.

Pyrate Principle XVII - Don't Be Afraid to Board the Hunted

1. Marine Research Society, *The Pirates Own Book*, p. 352-3.

Interviews and correspondence with Daniel Boyer, Director of Sales and Marketing, Vanderhall Motor Works, Inc. by Steve Monroe

Staying Moored in Your Home Port:

1. (Parade Magazine), September 1, 2017, p. 12, 15.

Bibliography

ABC Supply press release, May 12, 2016.

Angela Ridling Interview with Jessica Harman

Beery, Wallace, *Treasure Island* (MGM, 1934).

Breverton, Terry, *Black Bart Roberts The Greatest Pirate of All.*

Brooks, Baylus. *Blackbeard Reconsidered*, p. 43.

Burney,Teresa. http://www.builderonline.com. October 2012

Butler, Lindley S., *Pirates, Privateers, and Rebel Raiders of the Carolina Coast*, p. 13.

CNN Financial News Interview

Colonial Williamsburg Journal, Vol. 15, No. 1 (Autumn 1992), pp. 22-28.

Cordingly, David, *Under The Black Flag*, p. 108.

Defoe, Daniel, *A General History of the Pyrates*, second edition, p. 30.

Duffus, Kevin, *The Last Days of Blackbeard The Pirate.*

Exquemelin, Alexander, *Buccaneers of America*, 1678.

Fabor Report, April 5, 2017.

Harvard, *Hostile and Unsolicited M&A.*

http://www.abcsupply.com.

http://www.kentuckyale.com, www.alltech.com

http://www.investopedia.com/terms/h/hostiletakeover.asp#ixzz4dZfzGN8Z.

http://www.themarketedge.com

http://www.marketgraphicsresearch.com

http://time.com/money/4643435/super-bowl-patriots-robert-kraft/

https://en.wikipedia.org/wiki/Robert_Kraft

http://www.zappos.com

Interview and correspondence with Roger Clodfelter, Senior Vice President for Communications, High Point University

Interviews and correspondence with Daniel Boyer, Director of Sales and Marketing, Vanderhall Motor Works, Inc. by Steve Monroe

Johnson, Captain Charles, *A General History of the Robberies & Murders of the Most Notorious Pirates*, p. 55.

Hunt, Steve, interview with Steve Monroe

Kinkor, Kenneth J. "Bandits at Sea a Pirate Reader." *New York University Press.*

Kolak, Ben, Jean Yves Chainon, Guglielmo Mattioli, *New York Times*, August 7, 2017.

Konstam, Angus, *Blackbeard*, p. 251.

Lee, Robert E., *Blackbeard The Pirate*, p. 7.

Lewendal, Marilyn interview with Steve Monroe

Little, Beneron, *The Sea Rover's Practice*, p. 145.

Marine Research Society, *The Pirates Own Book*, p. 346.

Marx, Jenifer G., "Brethren of the Coast", Chapter 2, p. 36. *A Worldwide Illustrated History of Pirates*

McMahan, Dana. *Kentucky Monthly*. February 2017.

National Public Radio Interview, Studio 1A, August 7, 2017.

New England Pirate Museum, 274 Derby St., Salem, MA, 01970. New York Times, February 26, 2017.

Okuk, Niki interviews with Jessica Harman

(Parade Magazine), September 1, 2017, p. 12, 15.

Peter King Interview

(http://mmqb.si.com/mmqb/2017/01/30/robert-kraft-patriots-nfl-super-bowl-51-falcons-peter-king)

Providence Business News, December 3, 2015.

Rediker, Marcus, *Villains of All Nations: Atlantic Pirates in the Golden Age*, p. 151.

Ruesink, Megan, *Top Corporate Mergers: The Good, The Bad & The Ugly.* September 28, 2015.

Ryssdal, Kai. "Marketplace" NPR/American Public Radio. *Creating Jobs in Compton by Keeping Old Tires Out of the Landfill,* Garrova, Robert, writer. , 09 Dec. 2016.

Vallar, Cindy. Blog.

Woodward, Colin, *The Republic of Pirates*, p. 207.

Woodard, Colin. (2014, February).

http://www.smithsonianmag.com/history/last-days-blackbeard-.

Wanna Transform Yer Business or Organization?

Invite a Principled Positive Pirate aboard for yer next meeting/ retreat.

Learn Leadership Secrets that brought light to dark and desperate times and indeed transformed civilization. When applied, they brought out the best in women and men. Why not have a leadership/planning retreat that will be truly memorable and apply these secrets to yer world?

Sales? Watch what happens when yer sales team becomes a sales crew and uses the undiscovered resources at hand to approach their careers in a renewed fashion.

Customer service experience for yer customers will go to new heights of satisfaction once yer team forgets about team and becomes a crew, with new language that will transform the customer's experience with yer company or organization.

What did we miss?

Yer company or organization will experience power and passion that will come when the Pyrate Principles ™ crew works closely with yer leadership in designing a workshop, retreat, or planning session based on yer needs and wants. It will be the best meeting EVER! AYE!

Are ye serious about long-term application for yer crew? Our unique-one or two-day formats are designed with that in mind. In particular, day two is on water, using lessons learned in the classroom, plus experience with period firearms, cutlasses, and cannon. Applications that will be remembered. Contact us and watch yer horizon become clearer, more productive and profitable.

Depending on location, ye can share the wealth of new found knowledge as the Pyrate Principles ™ crew takes their positive message to elementary/middle school classrooms with a "Brethren of the Coast" session. This 50 minute experience for students, on yer behalf,

Contact Steve, Keri, or Jessica for a free consultation to address yer needs/wants:

stevemonroeenterprises.com 336-312-6754

Notes: